F*ck Your Excuses

By Ryan Stewman

Fuck Your Excuses

All Rights Reserved

Copyright © 2017 Ryan Stewman

This book may not be reproduced, transmitted, or stored in whole or in part by any means, including graphic, electronic, or mechanical without the express written consent of the author except in the case of brief quotations embodied in critical articles and reviews.

ISBN-13: 978-1544122557

ISBN-10: 1544122551

Cover design by Rob Secades

Contents

Chapter #1: The Power of Not Giving a Fuck 5
Chapter #2: The Secret to High Production 71
Chapter #3: Dealing with Your Demons 130
Chapter #4: The New You 180
Chapter #5: Upper Limits 218
Chapter #6: Relationships 251
Chapter # 7: Breaking Through Walls 286
Chapter #8: Happily Ever After 320
About the Author 337

OWN IT ACADEMY RESOURCES

To hear the complete audio recordings, please join Hardcore Closer's Own It Academy through our Facebook page, where you can also access each week's lessons and homework:
https://www.facebook.com/groups/oiacademy/
I hope to see you there!

Chapter #1: The Power of Not Giving a Fuck

Before you start this book, there are a couple of things that I want to get out of the way. I'm not a counselor. Whatever shit I may say, you need to ask your CPA, your legal advisor...ask somebody—a professional—how this stuff works.

I'm a gentleman who's been through a lot in my life. That's the only thing that's really qualifying me to write about this stuff. I've been through a lot of failed experiences that I've learned from. The whole reason I wrote this book is to help people avoid some of those experiences, or if you're going through those experiences right now, to tell you how to get through them.

The good thing for you and the weird thing for me is that I've been through so many experiences that we're going to be able to relate to a lot of things on a lot of different levels.

I often refer to myself as the luckiest, unlucky bastard on the planet. For every time that I have hit what I thought was rock bottom, there was always something a little bit less on the other side just waiting to twist the knife. I've had some really good highs, too.

Truthfully, the mindset has a lot to do with all of that. The people who join The Tribe, or come to Break Free Academy, find the sales and the marketing stuff is cool, and they get their leads, and they close them. But more importantly, it's the mindset behind what we do. We teach that it is the mindset of doing social media intentionally at Break Free Academy and Break Free Academy Digital.

That stems from me doing life intentionally. That's what I'm going to teach you in these pages—how to intentionally do life my way.

Again, I'm probably the least qualified person to give you this advice. I'm just going to give you the experiences I've had and how I've hard-headed my way through them. Because many of you reading this know like attracts like.

Many of you are hardheads just like me. You're like, "I need to figure this shit out, Ryan. Crack the code in some way or another, so I can figure out what it was that was that tipping point."

After I share with you the reason I wrote this chapter, I'm going to let you in on answers to questions I frequently get. And these questions, of course, will all have to do with this chapter's topic.

But first I want to address what not giving a fuck means. Not giving a fuck is the biggest problem we have because we give a fuck about the wrong things. We give a fuck about people's opinions of us that have no bearing in the marketplace, that have no bearing in our bank account, that have no bearing in any positive points in our lives.

As a matter of fact, we'll oftentimes try to please the people who give the least amount of shit about us. There comes a sort of freedom that you get for not giving a fuck that you can't get anywhere else.

I often say to my sales clients, "Listen, when you can generate your own leads, and you can close your own sales, you are powerful, and you can go wherever the fuck you want, get any job you want on this fucking planet. I'm proof." The same thing happens when you stop giving a fuck about what the sheep think, and you become a wolf. Then you'll start leading the pack.

Why do people give a fuck? Let's just dissect this shit back to the beginning. I'm going to break this down to what I think is the simple process of how we get to where we are, and how we get wired as adults.

Now, you have to understand, I've been through a lot of personal development courses, and I have a shitty attitude most days. You can tell by my posts on Facebook. I'm not Mr. Realism, but I get easily frustrated just like you. The fact is that I've decided not to give a fuck. I decided not to give a fuck to an extent so much that I don't have a license; I don't have a boss; I don't have a governing body that tells me what to do. Things have happened to me. So, let's go back to the beginning.

When we go to school, it starts to condition us to think a certain way. See, oftentimes, people *think* that school is about education. While it does teach us stuff, really what goes on inside of school is molding you to be a citizen. If school was about education, then they would teach us how to fill out our taxes. They would teach us how to work the legal system. They would teach us things that really mattered. These are things that we have to use as an adult, but they don't teach us any of that. They teach us a bunch of lies, to be honest with you. I'm not referencing a conspiracy theory, history lessons, or anything like that.

They teach us those lies so that they can socio-condition us to go into the workplace and become employees. If you have what Alex Charfen calls the Entrepreneurial Personality Type, the EPT, they label you as ADD. They tell you that you need medicine. All because a teacher decided to get this job for $40,000 a year, and you're not doing exactly what they say. The reason why they took that job for $40,000 a year is so they can exercise some sort of control mechanism over people who are weaker minded. That's just the bottom line.

They go in there and start teaching these kids how to behave a certain way, and they suppress the fucking behavior that's going to make them most successful in the future. It starts at a young age.

After you get reprimanded a few times as a kid for standing out, for saying something, for being funny in class, for having a faster answer than somebody else, forgetting to raise your hand or some stupid thing like that, they start to socio-condition you to be in the middle. They start to socio-condition you to be average. They start to say, "You shouldn't have beat Sally to the punch." Or, "You have to wait your turn. Don't be competitive. Don't be rude. Don't be pushy." They start telling you: "You might offend her," or "You might hurt his feelings." As a kid, you'd think an adult has their shit together. It's only when you reach adulthood, that you're like, "Holy fuck, nobody knows what the fuck we're doing here on this planet."

Teachers are people who are products of the system. I'm not knocking teachers. I'm not. I didn't have any good ones, but that doesn't mean there aren't any good ones out there. Chances are, many of you think about teachers like how you think about cops. If they were around you, you don't want them.

And teachers are institutionalized. I did three years of my life in prison. When you go to prison, you meet people who've been in there for 20 or 30, sometimes 40 years. It's fucking sad. It is what it is.

After a person's been in prison for about 10 years, they really start to lose the understanding of how the outside world works. Imagine if you'd gone to prison in 2005, and you've been in a prison right now for 11 years, you never saw Facebook. You have no fucking idea what social media is.

We call that institutionalized. These people are like dogs. They're used to getting up at certain times and doing certain routines. They've been doing that for over a decade. They become institutionalized.

Teachers are institutionalized. They have been in institutions their entire fucking lives. Again, I'm not knocking them, but I'm just pointing out the logic. From kindergarten through college, then back to the institution again. School is an institution.

They've socio-conditioned kids with lies that they have been institutionalized to believe. When we grow up, we're scared to offend people. We're scared to push forward for the sale. We're scared to speak up. We're scared to tell people who are not bringing value, who are not relevant to our lives, who don't make a fuck to fuck off. We try to please the losers, and we turn away from the winners. That's not a killer mentality, right? That's not what ownership's about.

You've got to move past the past. Pay attention when I mention the aspects of those around you. When I note teachers are institutionalized, that's how I want you to start thinking of other people who interact with you.

It's not that they're bad people or anything like that. They just don't know any better. Just like for those of us who are parents. I don't even talk to my parents anymore. We'll get to that in later chapters. But I find myself saying shit that my parents said to me as a little kid. I'm like *what the fuck am I saying*? That happens because we've been conditioned by somebody in our lives.

You've got to move past that conditioning, and we're going to dig into how to do that.

Consider this: When a circus act buys a baby elephant, they tie it to a stake in the ground. No matter how hard that elephant pulls, it cannot pull that stake out of the ground. The elephant pulls time and time again only to be disappointed. Eventually, the elephant grows big enough to be able to pull the spike out of the ground. It never tries again. The elephant's been held by something that could no longer hold it back, but it doesn't have the brain capacity or the risk tolerance to pull against it. People can literally just tie these elephants to chains, and they won't move because of the perception they are held down.

I'm going to make some bold statements as we move along. That's what's been done to all of us. That spike was drilled in the ground, and chains put around us at an early age. Right now, we have the ability to break through those chains because we are stronger than ever. Everything that you've done your entire life right up to this moment has been strength conditioning for you to break through that stake. You just have to have the mentality to take that risk one more time.

The past is what's holding you back. The more you think about the past, the more you think about mistakes, the more you let that spike, that socio-conditioning, hold you back, the longer it's going to take before you can be free.

By free, I mean in the sense of you don't owe anything to anybody, anywhere, at any time. I was in a meeting of some highly successful entrepreneurs one time. We were talking about joint ventures with people. I said, "I think these joint ventures would be great. I could get other people that have email lists, and I have an email list, too, so I could promote their shit. They could promote my shit. We could both help each other's audiences."

They said, "The problem with these JVs is if they make more money than you, or you make more money than them, then they start to feel like they owe you." I said, "Not with me because I'll make it 100 percent transparent up front of how this works. No favors, no anything. If they don't want to do it at that point, it's OK, because I have no fear of loss."

They said, "You know what? We never really thought about that. We've always just had the issues with them in the past." I said, "All it is, is setting expectations."

You have to set expectations with everybody whether you realize it or not. You have to set expectations with friendships, relationships, your kids and your employees.

A lot of people are stuck in the past. They have different expectations than you. Because they're stuck in the past, they're still held down by that spike, which maybe you are at this point, too. Hopefully, we can liberate that. But other peoples are still going to be held down by that spike.

We all know there's nothing you can do to change the past. The best advice that I can tell you is to say, "fuck it." The shit happened. It is what it is. Don't spend the rest of your life trying to solve something that doesn't really make a fucking difference. If you offend one person on this planet, if you lose one person, if one person's pissed off at you, there's fucking eight billion people on this planet. Somebody else will come along. You lose a client, fuck it. There's more. You lose a boyfriend, or girlfriend, fuck it. There's more. You lose a friend, fuck it. You'll find another one.

We get so attached. We have what my friend calls mental peptides. And these mental peptides come out in our brains. They are chemicals that make us feel good around other people, but oftentimes, they play a trick on you. As a man, you can say that other people's babies really aren't your thing. For the most part, they're not mine either. But you love your kids, right? Those mental peptides are playing mind tricks on you. If a grown man peed on you or did some of the things babies did, it would be on like Donkey Kong. You would be fighting them. But those mental peptides make you think whatever happened was cool.

People are out there holding onto their past. They're getting that mental peptide that's telling them "This is OK to continue to worry about the past..." I'm going to argue instead that there's nothing you can do to change your past, so I don't know why people worry about it.

I'm a prolific mistake maker. I've been to prison twice, divorced three times, been through bankruptcies, etc. I'm not going to name off lists full of shit that I fucked up on, but the fact is, none of it matters. I've already fucking done it. It's done. There's nothing I can do about it. If you want to use it against me, if you want to talk shit about me because of it, there's nothing I can fucking do at this point, because I don't have a fucking time machine. The only thing that I know to do is to block that shit out and just say, "Fuck it. It happened. So, what?"

My favorite line is "Don't act like you ain't ever done some dumb shit." I've just done so much dumb shit that I got caught a few times. Don't blame me for being a prolific action taker.

So, fuck it. People are going to come at you, and as you start to break free from this mentality, you start facing forward, and you stop worrying about the past, and you start worrying about the future. *What am I going to do next*, instead of *what have I done?*

The reason you struggle is because people want you in the past.

They want to bring you back. Those people that drive that stake that holds you back, they want to see you held back. They want you on their level. If they see you excelling, they hate. If they see you winning, they want you to lose. They start plotting against you. If you break free, then they fucking run out of excuses, too. Then when the world looks to them, and says, "Well, fucking John did it," they have to say, "Why haven't I done it? I'm better than John." Then they have to face the fact that maybe they're not. They don't want to have to admit that. They'll do everything to drive you back. "Oh, you're offendable. You shouldn't say that."

One of the biggest things that we talk about at Break Free Academy is what happens when people come in. I tell them, "When I teach you how to start posting on Facebook, your friends and relatives are going to ask you what's up with all the Facebook posts? They're going to say, 'You're some kind of professional now?' They're going to say all this dumb shit to you. Move past it."

People get upset, like my boys, Jackson and Asher. They foot race everywhere. They race to the elevator. They race to the car. They race everywhere, and each one of them will cry when the other one wins. That's the same thing. What's happening right now is you're racing your friends; you're racing your family. As soon as you beat them, they start crying.

Now, maybe it's metaphorical tears, in the sense that they start crying like, "Well, you shouldn't do that," or "Are you sure you're doing stuff that's legal?" "Are you sure you're helping people?" They start to instill these doubts in your mind, but just because they have doubts because of the past doesn't mean you have to.

Here's how you move past the past. First, you say, "Fuck it, it's happened," and you put some closure on that shit, and start moving forward. If you start worrying about being two steps ahead, instead of worrying about where you've come from, things will change.

The whole point of life is that it's the longest thing that we're going to do. We have to worry about what happens next. What's already happened has already happened. There's no going back and changing it. There's nothing we can do.

But what happens next is up to us. What's already happened may not have been up to us if you were a victim. It's easy for us to say as a victim, "I was a victim of the justice system. I was a victim of XYZ." I know. I was at the wrong place at the wrong time, so really, I wasn't a victim. I was a poor decision maker. I was a consequence sufferer, not a victim. I'll take ownership of that because I'm facing forward, and there's nothing I can do about what's already happened. All I can do is pat my chest and just say, "I fucking did that, so what?"

Dwelling on the past means you have regrets. But if you live intentionally, it gets rid of regrets. I'll explain what I mean.

I don't do anything on social media that I wouldn't do in front of the public. Now you're thinking, *holy shit, man, that's pretty wild*. Obviously, I'm not ashamed of anything. Lots of people do things they don't want to be public knowledge. They're scared behind bars because they're ashamed; they have regrets of what they're doing, but I just focus on the future and don't do shit that I would have regrets about.

Do I want to watch PornHub in front of social media? No, but I don't regret that shit. Do I want to have sex with my wife in front of social media? No, but I don't have any regrets there either.

I fucking have come to grips with the fact that there's just some natural shit that we all do that a lot of people feel guilty about, that we have regrets about. I don't. Some people might wonder: *even the smoking pot thing*? Do I have regrets about that? No. I enjoy it because I'm living intentionally. If I have regrets about it, I wouldn't fucking do it. If I were going to feel guilty about it, I wouldn't do it.

People feel guilty about stealing, lying and manipulating. I just don't do those things. I don't steal from anybody. I don't lie. If you don't like what I do, I'm not embarrassed about it. I've come to grips with it. You know what? I like to drink. I like to smoke, and this is me. I like to go out and party. I don't have a problem. If I want to watch PornHub, I'm a grown man. I can do what I want. If I want to go and have a drink, I can do what I want. If I want to smoke, I can do what I want. If I want to hop on an airplane, I can do what I want. You can't judge me, and your thoughts about that spike you have around your neck aren't going to hold me back from what I'm doing in life because I'm worried about the future, not anything else.

There are four things society uses to try to hold you back. When you become intentional about those four things, and knowing that they're out there, and knowing how they work, then you start to truly find yourself being free. If you watch any news sequence, always look for them. In any piece of political content always looks for one of these four things.

The first thing that society says is, "You're on drugs." We live in a time where marijuana is legal in multiple states. I'm not just talking about marijuana in itself, but drugs period. Cocaine, meth, X, etc.

We live in a time where a lot of people have done drugs, and it's pretty much accepted in society. It's not as taboo. Now, everyone is not going to walk around talking about the fact that they do drugs but weed is legal in a lot of states. People are on hydrocodone. The subject is more acceptable.

Some of the most popular people in the world talk about drugs. Celebrities, athletes, the Joe Rogans, those kinds of people own up to it, and it's no surprise. The thing is, it's 2016, and we're communicating more than ever. We have podcasts, videos, social media. We start to see that "Oh fuck; we're not as one-off, we're not as alone as we thought we were. I'm not the only one doing this shit. Fucking everybody's doing it. Maybe I shouldn't be ashamed?" Those thoughts start to come up for us.

Number two, people will say, "He's violent," or "She's violent." They think if you've fought somebody or hurt somebody, you have a history of violence.

The third thing is they say, "You're into weird sex shit." But who isn't? That's what we do as humans. We're all into one thing or another, and what's weird to somebody is pretty mild to somebody else. It just depends on your level of whatever the fuck you're into. Society, again, likes to hold you back. "She slept with him." "She's this, that." "She's a hoe, for sure." "She does this." Or, "Oh, he does this." Who cares if you're into weird shit? Maybe it's not weird to some people. If it feels good, who cares? You shouldn't have regrets. Many relationships are destroyed because of those regrets.

Number four, people will say, "He's racist," or "She's racist." These are the main four hammers that drive that spike into the ground and the ways that society will try to hold you back.

Now that you're aware of what society tries to hold against you, I'll explain how that relates to living intentionally. You just do your part not to have them hold those things against you. Obviously, racism is the most important of the four. Nobody wants to be called racist.

Again, the people who point the finger at you are usually the ones who are holding onto their own stuff. There's a lot to be liberated from.

The fact is that if you want to enjoy a drink, if you want to enjoy a smoke, then you can do whatever the fuck you want as long as it's not fucking up your life. I understand that some people have no self-control, and that shit happens. A lot of that is because of the mentality stuff I'm going to challenge you to work on, too. If you do have problems, I am not encouraging you to fall off the wagon, but at the same time, if you enjoy recreational use, you shouldn't feel guilty.

Some of the best podcasts and videos you'll ever watch have people talking about their experiences on drugs. Don't let society hold you back.

Living intentionally means that you won't do anything in the dark that you wouldn't do in public. I think that is one of the big things about Donald Trump right now, and why people are so drawn to him because he says the same shit onstage that he probably says offstage; he's very congruent. He's very confident. Whether you're a Trump supporter or not, that's not the point. The majority of the people out there have aligned with him, or at least the majority of the people in his party have aligned with him because he just doesn't give a fuck. He's comfortable in his own skin saying whatever. A lot of us equate that to using him as the example. We equate that to mean: "He's a billionaire. He's got that fuck you money."

It's not about fuck-you money. It's about a fuck-you attitude.

More importantly, taking it back to the beginning, it's about a not-giving-a-fuck attitude. Because with 10 billion dollars of cash, or assets, or whatever Donald Trump has, that spike's been broken. There's nothing holding him back. Pretty much any problem that he gets into, he can solve with money. He has that confidence. *Worst case scenario, the country hates me. I'm still worth 10 billion dollars.*

That's that killer mentality. Oftentimes, the people who are pointing the finger at Trump are people who wish they had the fucking ability to have that killer, not-giving-a-fuck mentality. Since they can't, they're the representation of trying to get somebody to suppress back down. This is the same thing that happens when your teachers try to get you to take your ADD medicine.

A lot of people are scared to be intentional. I watched a documentary one time about people over in Scandinavia. They were talking about their language being really, really vague. Their language came to be that way, over the course of doing battle over there, and through World War II, and World War I, and the French War.

Their language is this way for a reason. When they were questioned by people over the years, they could use very vague language and never get anything down precisely.

Here in America, we speak a very specific language, but I've noticed over the last two decades, our language has gotten vaguer. More and more people say shit like "I don't know," or "Well, you know." We have double meanings to words like we've never had before. Like good is bad, bad is good, right? The reason is due to fewer wanting to own up. They don't want to take responsibility, so they start to use language that's vague because it doesn't point them out specifically.

Here's why they're avoiding the intention. Because if people see that you have intentions, it changes the game. What do I mean by that? Here's an example. If you're driving down the street, and you spill hot coffee on your lap, then you swerve up on the sidewalk, hit somebody, and kill them, but it was an accident, you're probably not going to do time in jail. But, if you see a motherfucker that owes you 20 dollars, and you grab the wheel, and jerk up on the fucking curb and run his ass over, and you had every intention of hitting him, and then he happened to die, you're probably going to do a life sentence.

The difference was intention. Intention can get you in trouble. A lot of people know deep down inside they have fucked-up intentions, that's why they're so suppressed.

They try to do life unintentionally, or they try to avoid showing intention for the way that they do life. Not me. Everything I do is intentional, and if I didn't want to do it, I wouldn't do it. When I do something, I own it. I feel: *yes, I meant to do that shit, or I wouldn't have fucking done it.*

Rarely, do you hear me say, "That's not what I meant." Because I'm not scared to be intentional. When you do that people start to see you with renewed confidence. People start to say, "This is the guy that don't give a fuck." Yes, intentions come with consequences, but oftentimes, consequences are made-up shit in your mind that will never happen anyway. When you stop fearing consequences, you start living intentionally. People around you, start getting mad because they're still living these vague lives. After a while, here's what happens. They realize that you don't give a fuck, and guess what? They also realize that you don't give a fuck about their concern, and so they stop fucking trying to change you.

You see, they've been locked up in a prison of their own mind their whole lives. They've been told they have to do things a certain way; they bought into it. They've been told they have to be this way. They've been told they have to be that way. As soon as you stop behaving the way that they've been socio-conditioning you to behave, people will start freaking out and trying to get you back down to their level.

Here's another example. I live in Dallas, Texas. We're in the middle of the city. There's a very diverse culture around here. There are crazy crackheads at the store; there are homeless people just like any other urban area. When you go to the store, nobody's over there trying to tell the crazy crackhead how to live his life. Not even the guys who push the *Bible* shit, not even the Muslim dudes, nobody's over there trying to minister to the crazy guy and calm him down. You know why? They know he don't give a fuck, so nobody fucks with him. Nobody tells him what to do. Nobody gives a shit whether he does this, that, or the other. Whether he's acting a God-damned fool or any of that stuff because they know, he doesn't give a fuck.

You don't have to be the crazy crackhead at the liquor store, but there is a point when you should stop giving a fuck. People stop giving you their fucks, too. People stop saying they're concerned about you. They say, "It doesn't matter what you tell Ryan. He's going to do himself anyway." "It doesn't matter what you think about Ryan. He's not worried about that, and he's going to do what he wants to do anyway. You can't tell Ryan shit. That motherfucker don't care about your opinion."

Sure, it pisses a lot of people off because they want you to be like them. They're so held back; they want to hold you back, too. You're beating them to the elevator, and they're crying. You're beating them in the race of life, and instead of trying to run it harder, they just give up, stomp their foot like a toddler and start crying.

You can't let any of those people hold you back for anything you've ever done in your past. Because if you'd have done something horrible in your past, you'd be doing a life sentence right now. Trust me. I've met a lot of people in my life who have done shit that's horrible in their lives. They ain't ever going to see the good life again. They're never going to go home. They'll never be released from prison. You're not any of those people. Whatever you've done in the past, it's already over with. It's already happened. If it were something as atrocious as you think, it would probably hold you back. You'd be in prison for life.

We all fuck up. Those of us who make it past the fuck-up and get over it and start thinking two steps ahead, instead of one step back, and who don't allow society to tell them how to do life, will succeed. Your parents will stop trying to give you advice, and they'll start asking for advice. Does it happen overnight? No.

When you put the stance down, and you say *this is how I am, whether you like it or not, this is how I'm doing life, this is the mentality that I have...* you let go of that spike. There will be a lot of confrontations when you first let people in on your new attitude. It was a year before people finally said to me "Fuck it, man, he's real about this." Every person will go through their own period of time before people back down.

There's no half-step. You can't be on or off the fence. You can't try to appease people sometimes and then sometimes tell them to fuck off. It has to be a constant fuck-off scenario. A lot of people left my life in 2011 when I said, "Fuck it, I'm just going to be Ryan. I'm done trying to go to church and pretending to be that guy. I'm done hiding. I'm done trying to be a Mr. Positive motivational, inspirational trainer...like everybody else out there. I'm going to be fucking Ryan." The moment I said that a lot of people said, "Hey Ryan, you shouldn't be cussing in your videos." Fuck it. It's just me. That's who I am.

"Hey Ryan, you shouldn't be doing this, that and the other." Fuck it. We'll see. A lot of them left. Two years later, they started coming back as if they forgot that anything ever fucking happened. "Oh dude, I see you're super successful now. Congratulations, that's fucking awesome, dude." "Hey, how's the fucking wife?" I tell them "I divorced that chick. She's gone." It's funny to see it come full circle. They'll pretend like it never happened. Guess what? They know that whatever fucking words they have for you don't matter. It's not going to change your outline. It's just like arguing with someone over politics on social media. Whatever you say to them is not going to change their mind. If they support Trump, or Bernie, or Hillary, it doesn't matter. We're not going to change their fucking mind on social media. When people take that stance with you, and nothing that they say will change your mind with how you do your life, they stop trying to fucking tell you shit.

I don't get into political arguments with people because I know it's not going to change anybody's mind. That's the mentality you want people to have toward you. "I'm not going to tell Ryan not to cuss in his videos, because then he'll cuss twice as much just to fucking tell me to fuck off even more."

Here's the big part and before I tell you about it, you should know I'm not much of a hokey person. At the same time, the mentality about that steel spike that they use to hold you back is complete bullshit.

Ask yourself right now, who are you trying to please? Who are you letting keep that spike tied around your neck? Is it your parents? A friend? Your spouse? Are you concerned about a boss, pastor, co-workers? Why are you concerned, and why are you letting those people hold you back? Why are you concerned with what they think about you? Why are you concerned with pleasing those people?

Now, I'm not talking about everybody. We all have two or three people who we know we need to tell them what time it is. We need to say, "Fuck off, you're not in control of me. I'm tired of you fucking always coming around here with that bullshit."

Oftentimes, we refuse to do that. We tell ourselves, it's because we're nice, and we don't want to be rude. Isn't it rude of them to give us bad advice? Isn't it rude of them to hold us back? I'll give you an example. You know this is something close to me. It's a very painful moment in my life, and I wish that I could change it, but sometimes you just have to do what you have to do. That's all part of doing this life intentionally with a killer mentality.

In my book, *Hardcore Closer*, there are a lot of stories that only a person who does not give a fuck what society thinks about them could get away with writing. Let's just take a step back and consider rappers and actors. The things that they say in their songs and movies are what we wish we could do and say. Some of us have even lived those events but we can't talk about our experiences with people, so, we live vicariously through them.

In *Hardcore Closer*, I wrote my stories. Adoption, drugs, hookers, cocaine, prison, divorce. I wrote about it all. Troubles with my family, troubles at school. I remember my grandmother called me, and my father called me, and my other grandmother called me. They all begged me not to write my book. They said, "We're not going to talk to you anymore. You'll destroy our family, and people are talking about us."

My family comes from a town of about 2,500 people, and a lot of them are related to each other. I'm not even kidding. This is small-town Texas, and my family was worried about maybe 2,000 people in town who aren't related to them, talking about them when there ain't a house in the whole entire city worth over $200,000.

Oftentimes, people's tractors are the most expensive things they own. They're not people making huge dents in society. They're not world changers out there in this small town.

They're worried about other small-minded people from a small town, talking about them when they go to the post office, or wherever else. The truth is, my grandparents probably have the nicest setup and are some of the wealthiest people in the whole town, which is probably why they live there.

I'm not concerned with those people. I live in Dallas. I see people doing all sorts of crazy shit all day that they would never get away with in the small town where I'm from, or where my grandparents live. I lived there when I was very, very young. And in that small town, a lot of the things that we do here in the big city wouldn't fly because these people are so small-minded.

The reason why this story is relevant is because they begged me not to write this book. I had to cut them out of my life, and they chose to cut me out of their lives because of the book. It's painful, but I had to make that decision because my past could help other people. I've already sealed past it. I'm not worried about it.

They made the decision to move on, but. I said, "You're worried about 2,200 people in a small town that you don't even like, judging you for something that your grandson did. In the meanwhile, you're trying to keep me from sharing this story with millions of people who need it. Who need to be inspired by it, who need to hear it, and who need to be able to move past the shit that they're dealing with, so that they can understand I've been there, done that, and beat it. I can be the example for them. You're willing to rob millions of people of inspiration just to appease a few fucking rednecks that live around here?"

At this point, I don't know how many tens of thousands of

copies of that book that I've sold. I make a couple of thousand dollars a month from the sale of that book. The book is only $10, so you can do the math. We're selling a lot of them and have been for over a year now. The book has affected people. Every day, I get a half a dozen messages a day. "Man, I read your book. Shit changed my life." "I'm a convicted felon, and I'm now making XYZ money. I read your book." "It's just nice to see what's possible out there."

What if I'd have let my grandparents, people I love dearly, keep that spike around my neck? How much of an asshole would I be, and how much of an asshole would they be in all reality, robbing people—at this point, tens of thousands of people—more than that town times a hundred probably, population-wise, of a story of inspiration?

So, ask yourself this, who are you letting hold you back? What if I would have let them hold me back? We wouldn't know each other. That book's been the gateway drug for many of you reading right now. That book's been the gateway drug for many people in the sales pro group.

I get it. I love my grandparents. I still do. But I had to keep to my mind. It's like the power of not giving a fuck. I don't give a fuck what you guys are threatening me with. I'm on a mission.

I believe we're all given a voice in the back of our heads, and most of us try to drown it out with sex and drugs and alcohol. And I'm not suggesting that I'm fucking holier than thou. I just want to point out that I'm no different than you.

We spend our whole lives with this voice in the back of our heads. I remember the first time I heard the voice. I was five years old. By the time I was seven, they had me on medicine. All I was trying to do was listen to this voice. I started thinking, *maybe that voice isn't the voice I should be listening to? These adults who seemingly have their shit together are telling me that I shouldn't be doing what this voice is telling me to do.* Then I spent my whole life doing drugs, running, chasing things that didn't exist, causing trouble, going to jail, trying to silence that motherfucking voice. The voice is like that nagging girlfriend who won't shut up until I do what I am supposed to do.

You have a voice in the back of your head. It's been telling you your whole life you're supposed to do something. It's been calling you your whole life to take action, but you've let other people around you keep you from doing that. It may be starting a rock and roll band. It may be starting your own company. It may be doing arts and crafts on the side. It may be starting a charity. It may be creating your own corporation. It may be hiring that person and building that team. It may be starting that side project and pursuing your passion. Whatever it is, you have a voice in the back of your head.

We are all plugged into this grid here on Earth to provide a certain energy. What happens is when you start providing the wrong energy, it's kind of like having a bad spark plug in a car. The shit doesn't run right. The same thing happens inside our bodies. That voice in the back of your head was telling you to do something. If you're refusing to do it, and you're listening to somebody else who's not listening to their voice, and you're deciding to take that path, and you're deciding to listen to another human over the voice in the back of your head, you will never see the huge rewards.

I listened to that voice, and I spent my whole life all the way up till I was 29 years old avoiding that voice. I'm 36 now. My voice is as loud as a motherfucker. The voice told me to get out of the mortgage business; I told it to fuck off. The universe had to go so far as to remove me from society and put me in federal prison for 15 months during the mortgage meltdown.

Then, my dumb ass jumped back into the mortgage business, even though the voice was telling me to get the fuck out of it. It had to frickin' take my license away. Do I think that's all about me? No, I'm not that fucking narcissistic. But the universe has a weird way of working. I knew all along that I was supposed to be doing what I'm doing right now, helping people. Yet, I was making money doing mortgages, and the voice kept saying, "Dude, the fuck are you doing? You got bigger things than this fucking housing that you're working on over here." I'd argue: "Yeah, but the housing thing is paying me $300,000 a year, so shut the fuck up, voice. I'm trying to be busy living in my nice fucking house, driving my nice cars and shit, you motherfucker."

Then Dodd-Frank happened, and I lost my license. I started listening to the voice because I had no alternative. There was nothing else I could do. I lost my financial license. It removed me completely from the situation. I was a loan officer. I thought *fuck; this is the last chance scenario. I'll start listening to this voice.*

Guess what? I started listening to it. Things got harder. People, then weapons, and everything else it seemed, were formed against me. It wasn't all rainbows, and sunshine like a lot of people would have you believe. I lost a lot. I had to go live with my in-laws. Had to sell a lot of stuff and downgrade. I had to live within my means and borrow money from people.

But I listened to that voice. I got in alignment with it. I didn't get in alignment with it overnight, but it happened. And I realized every time I was borrowing money, every time shit wasn't right, it was because I'd deviated from what that voice was telling me.

That voice is plugged into your grid. It's plugged into the grid inside of your system, which is a universe unto itself. We're trillions of cells, just like there are trillions of stars in the universe. There are trillions of cells inside of us, and you're plugged into the grid. You're the actual plug into the grid here on the planet Earth. When you start listening to that voice, planet Earth will reward you. I'm not trying to be hokey, but at the same time, I'm telling you that voice is saying, "Hey, you're supposed to do this. Hey, this is your fucking mission on Earth."

If you spend your whole life running from that voice, and not doing what that voice is telling you and listening to what other people who are not listening to their voices tell you, then you live this fucking life of misery. That's why you're always in the past because you knew you should have done something else other than what you did. When you make that decision, you stay in the past.

Why do you care so much about these people that you're trying to please? What benefit are you getting other than that mental peptide, making you feel good because you listened to them instead of that voice? I can assure you this: when you listen to the voice, and you start training your brain right, those mental peptides are strong. So is the fucking cash that comes into your bank account. Even if you're doing benevolent charity work, even if you're starting a side hustle and shit, when you get in alignment, one of the rewards is not only self-confidence, and a not-giving-a-fuck mentality, but it's money.

This isn't a how-to-make-money book, but it is a fucking by-product. When you're doing the right things, and everything is in alignment, you're getting rewards. One of the biggest rewards you can get is money.

So, why do you care so much about those people? Why are you letting people in your life derail you, and detour you from what that voice is telling you to do? Why are you letting some shit you've done in the past hold you back? Why are you letting people hold it over you?

Once, when I was talking to Kevin Nations, he asked me what it takes to become an expert. I said, "I don't know, Kevin; 10,000 hours or whatever." He goes, "Nope. You just need to fly two states over and tell people you're an expert."

The people who love you the most will be the last people to trust you and the first people to hold you back. You could change the lives of complete strangers. I don't know anyone reading this book, other than those who have I connected to online, and through my training and social media. I haven't grown up with the people I consult with, or work with professionally. But a person I have never met would believe I was an expert faster than my own mama.

True story.

What if I was still trying to make her happy and she said, "You pretend you're an expert, but you're not"? I wouldn't be here trying to do my best for people.

When you listen to them, and you let them hold you back, why do you care so much, and what are you trying to prove by showing them that you care?

It doesn't serve you to listen to other people when it's a contradiction to the voice in the back of your head, and when you're not congruent. It doesn't take fuck-you money to become congruent; it takes a fuck-you attitude.

I don't mean that as a negative connotation where you want to hurt, disrespect, or belittle people or anything like that. If that's part of your shtick, then fucking fine. That's not the point. The point is saying, "Fuck you, I'm doing me." "Fuck you. I'm focused on me."

Oftentimes, we spend so much time focusing on the bad things that happen in our lives thinking "Fuck me and everybody else that gets the benefit," but we rarely say, "Fuck you." Again, I just mean words, actions and that spike around my neck have no bearing in my life anymore. I'm a grown elephant; I'm strong enough to break through now.

I have a friend who has a couple of sisters and a brother. They just don't have their shit together. They're adults. They're not successful. They went through college, and/or are still in college, and are grown. Just your typical haven't-really-made-it-much-in-society people. Not really bringing any value. Fifteen years in college, all sorts of degrees. Can't hold a job down, taking welfare. That kind of stuff.

My friend is talking about her family. Always going and seeing her loser brother and sisters. It hurts her feelings that they don't come see her, and she's worked hard to be successful. She's made all this money and has a successful life with kids. The family is always relying on her to come see them, but then her parents will always go see her loser siblings. I told her, "Listen, man, handouts don't come to hustlers. The people that don't have their shit together, it's easy for your family to feel bigger than them, to feel better than them. To be like, 'here's somebody in a worse situation. Let's help them. Let's lift them up.'" Meanwhile, you get fucked. You're on your own. They're like, "She can take care of herself," or "She can handle her own. She's going to be all right." "She's a survivor." "She's successful."

You just have to stop caring. They're probably not going to help you as you show that you're stronger, and you show that you give less and less of a fuck. The people who were holding you back will stop caring, too. They'll stop reaching out.

They'll stop offering as much help. That doesn't mean that they love you any less; it just means that they're starting to respect you.

At first, you can expect all sorts of opposition when you step out when you get congruent, and you listen to the voice in your head. Opposition only means that you have a breakthrough coming your way.

Let's recap on the mindset of someone who's relentless in their pursuit. The mindset of someone who doesn't give a fuck. The fuck-you mindset. This is what is involved in that. Not dwelling in the past, because the shit's already happened. If you're living life intentionally, it doesn't matter what happened. It's time to move on. Your mentality needs to take a shift from worrying about things that have happened in the past because if it were bad, you'd be doing a life sentence, but you're not, so you need to move on. Your mentality needs to make that shift from what's happened in the past to what's going to happen in the future. As soon as you stay focused on the future and on staying two steps ahead, and you start living intentionally alongside that voice for those two steps ahead; then the path no longer matters.

When you start thinking two steps ahead, and you start being proactive, instead of reactive, you stop having regrets because you had already thought out what was going to happen before it happened. If you've made the wrong decision, it was still intentional, and you just have to come to grips with that. You should still not have any regrets. If you did something intentionally, it's already happened. No matter what it is: good, bad, ugly, or indifferent. It's already happened. There's nothing you can change about that, so regrets are useless.

Live a life intentional. Remember the difference between the guy on the sidewalk. The deciding factor between the life sentence versus walking away was intention. We say this in our sales training, "When you're intentional with things, most people aren't." When you get on a sales call or post on Facebook, people don't realize that you're being intentional.

People are scared to be intentional about their decisions when it comes to buying something on a sales call. They've made so many bad decisions, and every time that they have been intentional, it's been a get-rich-quick program or the equivalent of big dick pills in the back of a *Penthouse* magazine. They're always falling for something that they shouldn't.

They've made so many bad decisions, and when you make a bad decision, it's easy to say, "I was uneducated." "Well, I didn't know," or "I just assumed." It's easy to not take personal responsibility. But if someone has intentions, they have to take personal responsibility. It's like standing up in court and saying, "Yeah, I ran over him. What?"

Most people don't have the balls, and they're scared to do that, so they live very vaguely and unintentionally. It scares the hell out of people when they see people like us, who are living intentionally, but we're living with the right intent all because we took our head off the past and our regrets, and we moved our head to face forward into the future. We're focused on staying two...not 200, not 2,000, not 20...but just two steps ahead and being intentional toward taking those two steps.

Don't be ashamed of anything that you do.

Now, you know that there are certain laws and there are certain ethics, and that voice in the back of your head tells you, *this is wrong. This right. Don't do the wrong shit. Do the right shit.* I know that sounds like, "Well, that's overly simple, Ryan," but think about this for a second. When you get to a point where you're not doing anything in private that you wouldn't do in public, or at least talk about in public, then you come from a place of congruency that's unheard of in this society.

So many people are ashamed of their past, and their actions, and so many people hide them. They shouldn't, but it's because of religion, or it's because of their parents, or it's because of their family, or it's because of their friends that they hide what they've done. You get to take action with intention. And when you do, you get to do things you are not ashamed of. People are drawn to that type of attitude.

Guess what? A lot of people repel from it, too. You may run some current prospects off. That simply means your future prospects will be better, and that's what you're supposed to be focusing on anyway. At no point, have I asserted you should focus on the now.

That's somebody else's book. My book is focused on two steps ahead. A lot of people say if you're worried about the future, you're anxious. Well, I didn't mean you should worry, motherfucker.

Listen, you doing what you want all the time keeps that shame away. You can ask me anything, and I'll fucking tell you because I'm not ashamed of it. Because if I'm ashamed of it, I wouldn't fucking do it.

What happens when you get in alignment and you use the fuck-you attitude is this: you're not scared to fail; you stop trying to please everybody; you start focusing on that voice and what you're supposed to do to serve your part in your mission in this mother-fucking universe. The struggle stops. I'm not saying the financial struggle stops, but the struggle, the inner conflict which is the real struggle—the struggle that all other struggles inside of every struggle that you've ever fucking struggled with—stops. Because the main struggle is the voice that's telling you to do something, and you're trying to shut the fucking voice up.

The voice is like that nagging girlfriend. She's not going to stop until you mow the yard, motherfucker. You can't drink her into shutting up. You can't smoke her into shutting up. She's going to fucking nag until that got-damned yard is mowed. It's your time to mow the yard, motherfucker.

That voice is going to be on you. You may think, *well, shit. I don't have a voice.* No, you've just gotten so good at silencing that motherfucker, you've tuned her out. You've gotten so good at tuning her out that you don't even hear her anymore. You need to start fucking listening. You got to because the struggle fucking stops when you do.

The first step's being aware. I know that I didn't put this chapter into any kind of Ivy League, long, drawn-out, psychology, you-need-a-fucking-degree delivery. Like I said, I have a very short vocabulary. We're very plain and simple and to the point here.

Now that you're aware, and you can start living intentionally, you need to start listening for that voice. For those of you who have been trying to make it quiet, you need to start figuring out what the hell it is that it really wants you to do.

When I first heard that voice, it told me that I needed to be a preacher. That was the only word that I knew of for that type of occupation—and it's what I do every day now. At 13-years-old, I knew. At 28-years-old, I jumped on the couch in the living room of my house like Tom Cruise on *Oprah*. I had no idea that any of the two correlated and said, "One day, I'm going to lead the world into world-changing shit. I've got these ideas, and these are the things I'm going to do alongside them."

Since then I have rid the word "preacher" from my vocabulary, but I still knew that I was going to be a world changer. Yet, I decided to do mortgages. Yet, I decided to do cars, and I couldn't understand why I kept going to prison. I couldn't understand why I kept getting in financial jam after jam. I couldn't understand why this wouldn't happen, that wouldn't happen. Until I started listening to that voice and actually becoming that "preacher." Then I understood why nothing else had worked.

Guess what? I've been listening to the fucking voice now full time for six years and have fully surrendered to that motherfucker like it is a demigod. I just bought a house for fucking cash; we have exotic cars. We live in a fucking penthouse. We're about to buy another house up the street to flip. We have money in the bank. We have a beautiful set of children. We have friends we hang out with all the time who don't care if we have money or not. That has nothing to do with it. Oftentimes, they buy our shit. We have a great staff of contractors that help support our team and grow our LLC that we own. All because I listened to that voice.

A hundred or so people have been expelled from my life. People who were there at one point saying, "Hey man, we've always been around. You're kind of fucking letting us down with this bullshit." They're all gone. Guess what? A million, sometimes three million people a week listen to my voice, read my blog posts and watch my videos. That replaced everybody who was fake. I had to get out of this real relationship. A lot of people were scared that I started keeping it real because they're like, "What if he tells my shit? What if he calls me out? Fuck!"

Guess what? It's been six years now, and there's nothing to call out about the people I've surrounded myself with. If I do, it's just a simple conversation that I need to have with them. They're like, "Hey man, you're right." And the same is true if they call me out for something. There's no more fake shit. The people that I have relationships with are genuine.

I've had fake relationships with spouses, and that's my bad. It's not theirs. I take ownership for it. But the relationship I have with Amy now is based on our reality. She knows everything. She read a book about my life before we even decided that we were going to get close. I operate with 100 percent transparency, so nobody can hold anything against me.

You'd think that the first thing my competitors would say would be "He's been divorced, bankrupt, been on drugs, and had a foreclosure. He got kicked out of the mortgage business. Why would you take mortgage advice from him? He's never had a real estate license. Why would you take real estate advice from him?"

I've already addressed all those things up front. I've already been like *what the fuck's that got to do with the fact that I know what the fuck I'm doing over here*? And I've sold more houses in my lifetime without a license myself than most agents will sell their entire fucking career—if it spans two decades.

I wrote a blog post on HardcoreCloser.com. She's a quick read, probably a thousand words or so. It's called "The Power of Not Giving a Fuck." Read it. Share it. If you dig it, pass it to somebody else. Then the next time somebody fucking tries to make you give a fuck, give them that blog in true not-give-a-fuck formation.

When you're done reading, make sure you answer these three questions, that we've taken directly from our Wufoo Strategy Session link, available in the Own It Academy group. You can also get to the link by searching Wufoo Strategy within the group page, or you can write down your answers using the questions here.

1. What three things have you struggled to get past?

2. What three people do you need to remove from your life?
3. What three things are you going to do for yourself?

Here's the point behind this exercise. It's about you putting those names into the universe. It's about you letting those feelings and those names out on that sheet. It's you filling the form out, using the words through your brain and letting them come out your fingertips. You're releasing that shit. It's a metaphorical release. You're releasing it from your brain, through your fingertips, and into the keyboard. You're releasing those names, but it also makes what you're doing real.

Yes, you can go around inside your head and pretend like this, that, and the other didn't happen. But when you type out the facts, when you put it on paper, and you send it out into the universe, that makes it real.

I want you to do this because that's how you're going to start the process of getting it out of you.

The first thing is getting it out of you, letting that brain and subconscious acknowledge these are the people, these are the situations, and these are the actions. When you do this, then you move forward.

In that spirit, I'll share with you some of the questions I've gotten that pertain to this chapter.

Q: "What are some rituals and habits I have implemented to keep my energy and enthusiasm up?"

It's especially hard to keep your energy up when other people are trying to tell you what to do, and they are dragging you down. The other day, I had an issue with another sales trainer. It was frustrating, and I let that person derail me for the day. But I didn't let it get my energy down. The next day, what happened the day before was in the past. There was nothing I could do about it, so I focused on staying two steps ahead of that motherfucker.

Here's some weird habits that I have that will help you out. Weird habit number one is, I listen to eight hours of affirmation on YouTube. I was telling Amy last night, "We're those fucking weird people. We made a little money. We live in a fucking nice place. We have fancy cars, and we listen to fucking positive affirmation shit. I'm the fucking douchebag that everybody makes fun of, and every fucking movie that starts out in Hollywood, right? I'm that fucking guy." And I get it. You know why Hollywood makes fun of those people? Because they don't want you fucking doing affirmations.

They don't want you breaking society. They don't want motherfuckers with a fuck-you attitude. They want motherfuckers with a socio-conditioned attitude.

Positive affirmations are phrases somebody says over and over again for eight hours. "You're awesome." "You have a huge penis." Those kinds of statements.

Onto the next question:

> Q: "They want to promote me to area sales manager. I feel like it will make me grow more. However, I know I will also lose a bit of freedom. What are your thoughts on when it's best to become a sales manager?"

What you need to think about in terms of becoming a sales manager is that you have to deal with other people. But if you're going to deal with other people, again, you're going to have to go through the I-don't-give-a-fuck attitude. There are going to be people who come on board, who are going to try to tell you how to do your business. But you have the experience. You have that voice in the back of your head saying, *you do have the experience, and I know what I need to do for the company.* You're going to be managing people, and some people will try to hold you back. There are going to be people trying to tell you how you could do a better job as a manager, but you just need that fuck-you-I-know-what-I'm-doing attitude.

I'm not really that good of a manager. I have four managers who work for me. Shit, I'm just the guy who creates content for my company. I'm a terrible manager. But how I handle it is what works for me.

Here's another question I've received.

> Q: "I feel like the voice is telling me to get involved in an industry that will not allow me to provide the life I want to give to my family."

This question gets right to the heart of this topic. What happens when your voice calls you and tells you to do something? Let's say the voice has called you to start a charity. I'll give you an example.

My ex-father-in-law is a great guy. I like and respect him a whole lot. He's been one of my mentors for a long time, and I still consider him that way. He's a great guy, and he's older than dirt now, about 77 years old. When he started a little charity called Children's Hospital, it was with the intention to help out local children who couldn't get insurance at the hospital. He and another guy started the movement and grew it. Then the other guy passed away and so the torch was passed on to my ex-father-in-law.

My ex-father-in-law told me, "I didn't get in this business to make money. I didn't get in this business to do anything other than help kids, and to provide for my family." My ex-father-in-law is extremely wealthy, and the Children's Hospital in downtown is one of the biggest buildings in all of Dallas. They've helped millions of kids by now. He was with the charity 40-something years, and they never fathomed in those 40 years that they would ever be what they grew into being. His voice told him to help kids. That's what he fucking did. Because of that, he got stupid wealthy.

You may not think the voice will provide for you, but like I've referenced, when you get in the right place with alignment, the universe rewards you. Not only with ending the struggle inside your brain; it will financially reward you, too. One of the biggest rewards that you could have in our society today is money. When you're in alignment, that shit just comes to you.

Now maybe there's a struggle. In my life, all you see before you didn't happen overnight. It took four years before we started seeing any money in this business from listening to the voice. There was a fucking time where I thought that I was going to be fucking broke forever. But at least I wasn't going to prison. In all seriousness, my situation was a bit more dire than most people.

You've got to provide for your family, too. When you're listening to the voice, there's always a way. It always shows up. When you're in alignment, what you need is provided for you. It's almost like faith, like what people would have you believe about religion. When you're in alignment, and you're not breaking the commandments, when you're following the prophet, when you're doing whatever it is that is your religion then you will be rewarded. Maybe not right away, but your rewards are coming. A lot of churches that I've been to teach about tithing and what you give out coming back to you.

I went to a church in Frisco, Texas. Before they'd give their tithes, they said something along the lines of "For this money that we're giving to church and God, we're believing in interest in income. We know that the check's in the mail." They believed they would find the money and that their debts would be demolished. It was about them taking an action, and a leap of faith, and then their action receiving a reward back from the universe—this was the principle of what they were teaching, prosperity. It's the same for you. You may not be able to follow the voice 100-percent but show the voice you're making progress and choosing to follow it. I'm telling you, things will fall into place.

Another good question that plays right into this subject.

Q: "How do you get over the fear of being broke?"

That's a good-ass question. Ask yourself this: is it a fear of being broke? Because broken can oftentimes be fixed. Broke doesn't mean dead. Or do you have a fear of failure? You can only fail if you lose. Many times, people equate being broke to being a failure.

They say, "I'm broke. I don't have any money. That means I'm a failure." Just because I didn't have money in 2012 when I was starting the Hardcore Closer business, doesn't mean I was a failure. At the time, I thought of myself as one.

Guess what? I did anything to act like I wasn't a failure. I did what they call the fake-it-till-you-make-it type-shit. I wasn't faking it about that. I had money and stuff. I was faking it with a positive mental attitude. I was trying to be like the Joel Osteen of the sales world.

Listen, we don't need another one of those guys. There are plenty of them out there. They've been around since the dawn of time. The sales world needed someone like me to be real, to listen to that voice.

I was broke, because I was failing, and I was failing because I wasn't listening to the voice. If you have a fear of being broke, it really means you have a fear of not listening to that voice. You might think, *man, this guy's gotten hokey as hell*. This is why I don't share this shit on my sales training. This is why this is separate.

If you're listening to the voice, it will provide for you. And broke doesn't mean you're a failure. Maybe you have to downscale. To get where we're at now, paying cash for houses, etc., I had to live in the extra bedroom in my in-law's house. I had to sell two houses that I owned.

Don't get me wrong, neither one of them were mansions. Both of them were $1,000 a month in mortgage payments for 30 years. They were assets that I had built, and like a missionary, I had to unload them. I had to fucking sell all my shit, and head out on a mission. Sold everything I had and took off for Jesus.

Guess what? I went all in. There's something to be said for going all in. I recorded a story about one of my clients the other day. It essentially covers the point that there are weird actions your subconscious will take if you act right.

My buddy is a great dude. He's been through the struggle, though. He's got this voice in the back of his head that's telling him to do something. He's tried everything in the world from heroin to alcohol to get it to go away. And we've all been there. I'm not judging him at all. I love the guy. He's one of my longest running friends.

He'd been on a downward spiral, and an upward spiral, and a downward spiral. He hadn't really seen the upward side of that spiral since 2005. He bounced around from job to job from 2005 to 2014. Finally, he landed a job over here at Perch, across the street. It's a retail place. For two years, he built a pipeline. One day, he came to me and said. "Man, I'm tired of fucking around. I've been trying to do this shit my way for 10 years. But for the last two years, I keep staying in the same fucking place. There's no moving forward."

I said, "Here's the thing, man, you just need to do XYZ." I gave him a little bit of personal advice. He said, "No, man, I'm talking about I'm going to buy your sales program." I said, "No shit?" He's like, "Yeah, the $500 one. I don't have $500." I thought *he's been down on his luck*. He continued, "I don't have $500. But I got a credit card with a $500 limit on it. I'm going to put it on the credit card. I don't want any discounts. I want to buy this shit, I'm going to learn it, and I'm going to fucking dominate my work. I'm tired of this shit. I'm sick of the struggle, bro."

I thought *fuck it. If he wants to buy the shit, then awesome. It'll work for him if he'll listen to it. Maybe he'll listen to it.*

Well, what happened in his brain right then is the same thing that happens when you listen to your voice. His voice told him that he needed to get my training. It was time to quit fucking around and get my training.

He bought my training. What happened next subconsciously is what changed the game for him. He listened to that voice that told him he needed help. He got that help. He put the shit into play. His subconscious said, *you just took a bet on yourself.*

When you listen to your voice, you take a bet on yourself. You say *you know what, voice? You're right. I'm going to do what you're telling me because I believe you're right.* That voice is in your subconscious, and when you listen to it, you're betting and believing in yourself, which boosts your confidence.

My friend put down $500 that he didn't have, that made him stretch, that made him believe in himself, and it shut that compartment off inside his subconscious. It said *you know what? You just bet on yourself. You just believed in yourself. You just took a chance on yourself. You just put some confidence in the confidence bank in your brain, and guess what? We're going to reward you for taking action.*

Flash forward two months, and I hadn't heard from my friend. He's like any other client who buys the program. I don't track you down to see what your results are. Eventually, he reached out to me and said, "Hey man, I'm number one in the entire nation. Beating the boys in Tribeca, beating the boys in Los Angeles. I'm number one. We just closed a $2.6 million deal." He's like, "Man, your sales training changed the game for me."

I thought *my sales training ain't shit. What happened was you fucking went in on yourself. You went all in. No regrets. Focused on two steps forward, 100 percent in. Believed in yourself, built confidence up in the confidence bank in the back of your brain. Now you're fucking crushing it. It's no secret. It's not my sales training, while that probably helped you with sales tracks, and all that other stuff, you're in alignment with what you're supposed to do right now for your time.*

That's what I'll challenge you to figure out. It's not a fear of being broke. My friend was in fear of being in debt. When you show your subconscious that you don't have fear and that you believe in yourself—like the people do who make the most money from multi-level marketing—you have to realize the client is not sold on the product. They're sold on their mission. They're sold on the solution.

Another question I've received:

> Q: "I work in an industry where basically everyone is Mormon. I could tell their stance hurts me a bit. How do you deal with not giving a fuck, when you know advanced opportunities could be jeopardized, like a manager's position?"

A no-fucks-given attitude doesn't necessarily have to be portrayed as if you are a mean person or a rude person. You don't have to be vocal like that. You just have to have a certain mentality about it.

I'm vocal about it because I don't have any governing bodies.

I don't have a licensing bureau. I don't have a boss; I don't have a manager. Whatever your circumstances, you have to keep that mentality, although that doesn't necessarily mean that you have to be vocal about it. You don't need to post crazy shit on Facebook or anywhere else.

I've had plenty of people over the years misconstrue what I'm saying.

But my not-giving-a-fuck is different than your not-giving-a-fuck. The things that you do give a fuck about, I might not give a fuck about. For example, I had to go to Utah Valley College and deliver a speech to a bunch of college Mormon kids not too long ago. They asked me not to cuss. As a matter of fact, they made me sign an agreement saying if I cussed, I had to give my fucking money back. All right. I signed the agreement. I can control my tongue if I need to and did like a fucking boss.

I was still able to portray my no-fucks-given attitude, to deliver my powerful sales training without cussing. I was able to change the message to match the messagee. I changed the message, so it fell on the right ears for the audience because if I'd have gone up there and cussed and talked about drugs and all the other shit that I normally do...it's part of my stand-up sales comedy routine…it would have fallen on deaf ears. That's because my audience wouldn't have understood it. I had to craft the message to hit the right person.

Here's an analogy. What if people were trying to convert you over to being a Mormon, and you could give two fucks about that? That's the attitude that you need. You don't have to be rude about it. You don't have to be mean. You just have to know that no matter what they're trying to put on you, you're not concerned with it.

It's not that you have to portray to the outside world that you're a badass or a tough guy. If anyone is trying to hold you back with some bullshit, maybe you don't need to go announcing inappropriate things. Let's say that I don't know the whole Mormon religion that well. Let's just say that Mormons aren't into sex. You don't need to go into work announcing on Monday that you're fucking having anal with your old lady in front of everybody. But don't feel regretful for that shit, either.

Sex is a big thing to a lot of people, or they're repressive about it. Don't feel regretful about it. Don't be ashamed.

The last question someone sent to me is really a four-part one.

Q1: "What clicked or what was the turning point when you said, 'Enough is enough. You either like me, or you don't,' without changing the essence of who you are?"

The biggest point that clicked for me was probably the turning point with my grandmother.

But another period of my life I can't forget concerned a gay dude I had met. The fact that he is gay is an important part of the fucking story.

He was a flamboyant ass. Imagine a flamboyant fucking gay guy and me running around together. We were like the odd couple. He was a really brilliant dude. The thing that I liked about him was he possessed an attitude of zero fucks given.

If you didn't like gay people, he didn't care. He wasn't running around trying to tell you to be offended, or trying to change your mind about gay people, or the fact that he liked dick or any of that. He wasn't trying to change anybody's mind, and he didn't give a shit what you thought about him. He was what he was. Pink hair, weird dude, flamboyant.

We both did social media stuff together for a real estate company and ended up being business partners in a little social media company. He lost his way at one point. That shit happens. The voice told me that I had to let him go. He was there in my life for a reason. The reason why was he'd given me some priceless advice. He said, "You've got to be you. People are going to judge you, and they're going to make an assumption about whether they like you or not—who you are and everything else. You're not going to be for everybody. There are eight billion people in this world. You've just got to be you. Some people won't take you and some people will."

I thought about that, and it was coming from someone for the first time in my life who was 100 percent them.

A lot of people say you have to be yourself all while they're pretending to be somebody completely different than who they are. This guy was 100 percent who he really was, and it made sense for the first time in my life. I saw somebody, strange as that motherfucker is, who was 100 percent congruent, and 100 percent comfortable with who they were, bullshit and all. Drama, gay, weird sex shit. All the fucking stigma that society held against him. He didn't give a fuck.

He lived a pretty powerful life doing whatever he wanted to do. So, that's when he gave me that revelation.

Q2: "How do I keep focus and not get distracted by negative

noise?"

I don't. I'm not a personal development guru, expert. I'm just some dude. Negativity distracts me like anybody else.

These are the facts about negativity. We have this thing in our brain called the amygdala. We're more prone to fight or flight than we are positivity. Just because positivity is like, *cool, high five. There's no threat there.* Negativity is like, *oh shit; it's a threat.* We're taught to go into panic mode because of natural instinct. We're naturally inclined to go into panic mode when confrontation or negativity comes up. I fall into this as well.

I don't dwell in it. The shit happens. Somebody said something bad. A dude's been posting some dumb shit online the last couple of days. I don't even know this guy. He joined our group, and he's frickin' being a troll in there. I said, "Leave him in because his negativity is hilarious. He gets to watch us work. While he's over there being negative and hating, he gets to see us make millions." It's great.

When it comes to negativity, I'll let it distract me. I'm not perfect, and it does distract me, but never more than a short period of time because I don't dwell in the past. *All right, shit happened. I'm over it. Let's move on.*

Negativity almost always comes from the situation you're in right now, or it comes from the past. If you think about it, there's no negativity in the future. You're not focused on being negative two steps ahead. If you are, you're a deviant, dammit. Stop that. That's reptile behavior.

In all reality, negativity can only exist in the past. You've just got to move past it. Oftentimes, the negativity comes from the social media outlets. You have to be quick to block people. My block list on Facebook's like 400 people. We have 600 people blocked in the sales talk group alone.

Out of all the billions of people in the world if one is being negative, remove them or replace them with a positive person.

Sure, it's going to distract you. Sure, it's going to piss you off. But move forward. If you realize that you're still thinking about an event from an hour ago; it's time to move two steps forward again.

Q3: "How do you stay competitive and not get lost in comparing yourself to others?"

That's really easy. You compare numbers to numbers, instead of yourself to someone else. It's that simple. When I compare myself to the number one sales trainer guy out there who's got almost a million fans on Facebook, I look at the numbers. He's got a 27-year head start on me. He has a million fans on Facebook. I've been doing this for four years now, and we have 100,000. He's got 27 years, and only 10 times the head start. I'll catch him in three years if things are done on the same scale that they are now.

I'm comparing myself, and I'm actually ahead of the game, and I'm doing better. But if I were to look at other considerations besides the numbers, characteristics and training programs, then I would be comparing myself to what's not real. I'm always looking to compare myself to the facts. If you're going to compare yourself to somebody else, you can't say they're a good guy because you don't know. You're not inside his head. The dude you are sizing up could be a fucking psycho who's completely in control of himself most of the time but could burst at any minute. You can't make assumptions like that. So, only look at the numbers.

Sometimes if you're getting beaten by somebody, you might feel like *man, their numbers are beating me across the board.* In that case, step your numbers up. Don't compare yourself to the person; compare yourself to the numbers.

Q4: "How do you keep focused and energized physically and mentally?"

I work out. Garrett J. White taught me what he calls the four-core: body, being, business, balance. These are the four areas of your life you must take care of. Your body means you have to work out. Try to take care of your business. You've got to make sure you're working it. You've got to make sure you take care of your bank account. You've got to make sure you take care of your family.

All that requires work and a lot of energy, so exercising is huge. A lot of us don't want to exercise. I'm not a health and fitness nut, but every time I'm anxious, or every time I'm low on energy, or lethargic, if I'll go workout, I'll get things flowing because I move things around. When that happens, then my energy starts flowing.

The way to keep energy is to create energy. One of the first websites I ever bought was called The Energy Producer. That was my nickname. I'm The Energy Producer. Because I'm going to continue to produce energy. The way that you produce energy is by taking action.

So, exercise is one of the things that's helped me really create a lot of energy and stay focused. Exercise is not easy. There are days you wake up, and you're like *fuck, I'm tired*. Exercise moves that tired around. It beats that tired's ass. It makes that tired go away. And it makes you feel better when you exercise. There's something to be said for the mental capacity behind it. It makes you feel powerful. It makes you feel good. It makes you feel confident. It makes you feel good about yourself, and that just leads into better consequences.

When you exercise, and you don't give a fuck, It's a winning combination.

Before you move ahead to the next chapter, and because I want you to use parts of this book like a workbook, read the not give a fuck blog post on HardcoreCloser.com and then start putting what you learned into practice.

Chapter #2: The Secret to High Production

There are secrets to being a high producer, things nobody tells you; nobody told me. I'm sharing from experience. I'm not going to blurt out a bunch of hypothetical stuff I've read in books.

In this chapter, I'm just going to tell you what's worked for me. Here's the cool thing about me, I'm like the luckiest unlucky bastard on the planet. If this stuff has worked for me, and I've been able to see some sort of degree of success through it as well, then it will definitely work for you. I'm just saying it because I have terrible luck. There are a lot of things that work for other people that don't work for me. These things that have worked for me have to work for you because again, the whole unlucky lucky bastard thing.

There are truly secrets to being a high producer. These are things nobody else tells you about; these are the things that I've never seen in books. These are things that come from my personal experience. But before we go any further, let me explain what a high producer is.

There are two types of people in this world: there are energy producers and energy demanders. Think about it like any country that we seem to have gone to war with. For example, you can use

OPEC and the others that provide energy—Tesla is a good example of a company that has actually turned the sun into a way to provide energy. When you're an energy provider, you get paid. That's what made Rockefeller worth a trillion dollars because he figured out how to tap into energy. That energy came from oil, but it's energy nonetheless. Well, these days, energy can come from software. Energy can come from within you. An energy producer or a person who produces energy for the energy demanders (the consumers—because we don't produce oil, we don't produce gas, but we consume it) demands the energy from the producers, except for my neighbors who drive Teslas; they command the sun.

Energy consists of all sorts of stuff. You've got the guys that are the Fortune 500 CEOs; they produce energy. Right when you first spot them, you might say, "Man, when that guy walks into the room you can feel the energy." You know that scene in *Boiler Room* where Ben Affleck strolls in, and he's talking about being rich and having a Ferrari and is smiling ear-to-ear? Clearly, he's got an energy about him. He's producing enough energy to roll up the rest of the guys in the boiler room. At some point, we're all energy demanders, too, and the key to life that I've found to be successful is to spend the majority of your time producing energy and as minimal an amount of time consuming energy as possible. Now we have to consume energy, right? We have to be an energy demander at one point or another because as an energy demander, we have to have food. Food provides us with energy, Red Bull, Monster, some people do drugs, whatever. I'm not a drug guy, but I'm not here to judge. People look for all sorts of stuff for energy, and I've done it, and I've looked at those options for energy, too.

I've had this drive my whole life. Just tons of energy pent-up inside me. They would say, "Oh, he's hyperactive," or "Oh, he's got this," or "Oh, he won't stop talking in class," or "Oh, he seems like he has a freaking comeback and an answer for anything." It was held against me.

Here you are, you've got all this energy, and they try to put you in sports. Maybe some of you are good at sports. I wasn't fortunate enough to be that good, and it's because I wasn't sure what to do with my energy. I know I didn't just want to run around and hit other people and throw a basketball. It was fun, but I didn't know what to do with the energy. I had all this energy inside me, and my energy, it turns out, strangely enough, is the ability to reproduce knowledge really fast.

It was funny that no coaches, no teachers, no parents, no one picked up on what I needed. I had all this pent-up energy, and it got me in trouble at a young age. I'm sure many people have gotten into trouble, and your issues managing your energy may even be causing issues at work. You're the high-energy guy there. People hate on you. Your boss doesn't like it because he's not high energy. Low-energy people or energy demanders and low-energy people, they don't like us. Because we're an example of *oh shit, what if you turn it up a notch and you're like this guy*? Most people don't go through life wanting to turn it up a notch. Most people go through life trying to have as much chill as possible (to sound like you youngsters. Trying to get the lingo down here). They go through life trying to chill more and produce less. Chill more and use energy less. Which leaves a wide-open gap for energy producers to run through.

I'd like to believe everyone who's reading this is an energy producer more than an energy demander, on some level. You're putting your energy toward digesting this information, so you can clear your mind to direct that energy somewhere else. The high-producer mentality is an energy producer. This is a person who produces energy at a higher rate than they demand it. Again, we've all got to demand energy. We all need help from somebody. We all need gas. We all need food, not like the gas that you pass but I guess that's a kind of energy, too. I was just working out my oil and gas and food together, and I'm sure that seems funny, so I left it in.

I'm breaking this down into three different sections, and then you have some more homework. Remember, how you show up in one place in your life is how you show up every place. So, do your homework!

I'll never forget when I was with Garrett J. White at Warrior Week in 2014. I was Warrior number 13. I'm an OG in a lot of these really cool people's programs because I'm an early adopter. I have a wrist issue. My wrist has broken three times, and the third time, the doctor said that they needed to put in a 6-inch rod and fuse it and after they did that my wrist doesn't move. There's no limp wrist over here on my right hand. It's like a 6-inch rod in my hand. I get that there's a big dick joke behind that, but my hand doesn't move regardless. So, when I was working out at Warrior Week, they had us doing something called double unders, which is a form of jump rope where you swing the rope twice under yourself in one jump. When you don't have any wrist momentum, you have to use your whole fucking arm to swing the rope.

I swung this rope, and I just couldn't do it, so the only other alternative to do it was 50 double unders or maybe 100 double unders; that would equate to 200 regular jumping jacks. Jumping rope was really hard for me to do. But I pushed through, and I got last place out of everybody in that exercise. I'll never forget,

Garrett and Christopher and John walking up to me and saying, "You know you got last place, but you finished, and you worked three times harder than everybody here in this competition. That's how you're showing up in your life." They're like, "We see it. This is one little exercise. But this is what it represents that you do. You finish. Sometimes you finish last, but you worked 10 times harder than everybody else around you." It's true. I want you to think about that. Those are my results, and that's why I've gotten where I'm at because I'm willing to finish and I'm willing to work harder than anybody else. A few times I've been able to win with that mentality. Sometimes, it hasn't served me very well like the jump rope incident. The reason I tell that story is because if you didn't do the homework from last week, and you're thinking about not doing the homework this week, where else is that showing up in your life? I've put homework in this book to specifically help you move through all the internal work you chose to do by picking up this book.

Let's talk about the high-producer mentality. The energy producer, the person who produces more energy than they demand, what goes through their mind and what allows them to produce that amount of energy? You've got guys like Steve Jobs, obviously passed away; Mark Zuckerberg is another example; Dan Bilzerian is another example. It's weird to use the three of them in one sitting, but if you notice those guys wear uniforms every day. I read an article one time talking about Zuckerberg and Jobs; they just wear the black mock T-shirt. That's their go-to and the reason why is because they have so much stuff on their minds that they don't want to cloud themselves with trying to decide what clothes to wear. That's just one less decision and one unimportant decision they have to puzzle over. Those guys are obviously high producers. For Dan Bilzerian, it's easier to throw a black shirt on, and some khaki shorts and then say *I'm good*. That's what he's known for: saying, "I don't have to dress up for anybody, so why spend time and mental energy on that?"

Think about the places where you're spending time and mental energy, and I'm not telling you to become a socialist and wear a freaking uniform. I'm just thinking out loud that if these guys are so focused on their time and so focused on their brainpower, and so focused on only making decisions that matter and they are some of the wealthiest people in the world, you should probably think about doing the same. There's a lot to be said, too, for the CEOs who are also some of the wealthiest people in the world who wear the same white and black suits or black suit, white-collared shirt every day. There's something to that and the reason why is because they don't want to have to make any more decisions than necessary; they don't want to spend extra time on what doesn't matter. Every second is precious.

When I was with Alex Charfen last week, he was talking about traveling with these multi-billionaire clients of his, on private jets, and going into hotel rooms. Once there, they all have water filter systems, and they all eat healthy, and he's like, "They're all worried about their health." I said, "Maybe that's not what it is. Maybe they just know that they're so important and they produce so much energy that they have to be at optimal health because if they die things could fall apart."

Look at Steve Jobs. He died, and Apple hasn't come out with a kick-ass product since he's been gone. The watch, sorry if you're wearing one, but eh, if that thing weren't made by Apple, nobody would wear it, just sayin'. There's a different line of thinking that goes along with being a high producer. If you're going to produce more than you demand, then you have to be different than the average person because the average person demands a lot more than they produce. Think about the minimum-wage workers who want raises. Minimum wage was like $3.95 an hour when I was a kid. I don't know what the hell it is; I think it's like $7.50 now. And these guys are demanding $15; they're energy demanders. You can't think like them. We have to start thinking like these big-time energy producers. Let me share with you what goes through my mind, the first thing every day when I wake up. This is the first thought that hits my mind as soon as I wake up... I look over at the clock on my nightstand, and I make the decision. You see, I haven't had an alarm clock in 10 years probably. I've set it a few times when I have early flights on airplanes, but I still haven't needed it.

I look over at the clock, and I have to decide if it's time for me to get up yet or if should I go back to sleep. Sometimes I look over, and it's 3:30, sometimes I look over, and it's 4:30, and I'm still not ready yet, but I wake up. That's my mind saying *hey, we've rested enough. We've demanded enough energy, Ryan to where it's time to start producing again.* I'll wake up at 4:35, no later than 6:30, and oftentimes, I'll sit in the bed really awake, just letting my mind get right because there's something you should know about what you do first thing in the morning. I read a book by Hal Elrod called *Miracle Morning,* and it's a decent book, but sometimes you can read a book, and you make a serious self-discovery. I realized through the book that the morning sets the pace for the entire day. How you set up your morning is how you set up your day. The way that you start programming your brain in the morning is important to how it's going to last you throughout the entire day. That's what I took away from the book, and I realized I've subconsciously been laying out my day, but I never consciously drew the conclusion from it until I read the book.

First thing in the morning, I read something positive. I used to wake up and read emails, or comment on Facebook posts, or scroll through my newsfeed on Instagram. A) it's just a bad idea to look at the screen first thing in the morning. B) it fucks up your eyes. It does. There have been studies about it. If you first look at your screen when you wake up, it causes long-term effects. If you look at something rather bright, it's like somebody switching the light switch on you. I want to start my day out with some positivity. In my line of business, not everybody likes me. Surprise, surprise. I get called a douchebag probably more times than your average person, and maybe I deserve that, but maybe I don't. I don't know. I'm not looking on the outside looking in, but I've grown used to it. I know I'm going to face those obstacles every single day. I'm not in denial. I'm self-aware. I know these obstacles are also going to hurt my ego, and they will get to me. It doesn't matter how many times I hear "Don't let it get to you." It still sucks.

I have to deal with people discrediting my shit. Telling me that I'm a rip-off of somebody else and it's just part of the job. Maybe there are other stressful sides to your job. Maybe you're a real estate agent, and your contract didn't get accepted. You know Donald, my real estate agent, had to write like four damn contracts and fight with me on every one of them before we finally got one accepted. Maybe you're a loan officer, and you know at one point, loans are going to get denied. There will be stupid conditions the underwriter last-minutes you on. These things happen; we know that whatever our job is. Negative things are going to happen, so why not prepare your brain and arm it with some mental floss, and some mind vitamins, so when the negative stuff comes up, you've already built up your positive account.

Think of your brain as an account. If you pack positive knowledge in there regularly then when negative and stressful stuff happens, you've still got enough positive resources upstairs to stay upbeat. I know it sounds hokey, but shit it works. There are a lot of things that sound hokey that work. You know who says it's hokey? Average-ass people scared to try something new because *what if it works and their fucking excuses are gone?* That's who says shit's hokey. They go, "That sounds like some hokey ju-ju fucking bullshit. It's Voodoo." What I am telling you works, but it doesn't work for average people because average people don't do it and if you did it and heaven forbid that it worked, then you'd have one less excuse of why you were a failure in life. That's what I think when it comes to people who say stuff like that.

Tomorrow morning, when I wake up, I'll roll over, and I'll probably read four or five pages, of a book by Joel Osteen. I know you're thinking *what in the living hell? Did I just hear Ryan Stewman say, he's reading a book by Joel Osteen?* Yes, because it's positive. I'm not reading one of his religious books; this one covers how to become a better you, and I'm sure it's going to have a lot of religious undertones, and that's OK because there's a lot of positivity. If you are a Christian, there's nothing wrong with that. One of the best things you can do for your life if you're Christian or even if you're not, but you're bold enough to take the step, is read a proverb every single day. In the *Book of Proverbs*, in the Old Testament, in the *Bible*, there are 30 different proverbs. You can basically read a proverb every day, and you might read the 30th proverb or pick another random proverb on the 31st day for those months that have 31 days. You'll get off a little earlier, or maybe you have to read two a day for a couple of days in February. Christians would call them biblical principles, but they're just principles that govern your life because Solomon was the wealthiest dude ever in the history of the planet.

Don't you think you could learn a few things from one of the two books? I believe there's two. I know he wrote Proverbs and I believe he wrote Ecclesiastes; he may have written a third one, but those are the two that I know that are in the *Bible* that he wrote. Those are books that were left from a guy worth hundreds of billions of dollars; that's an estimate. He set up trade with countries. He cut deals with Cleopatra. They were mining diamonds, gold and riches back and forth. He had a harem of over 600 women; he was the wealthiest man ever to live. Nobody, not Rockefeller, not Steve Jobs, not Zuckerberg, not Gates, none of those guys have what King Solomon had at one time. He had a massive, massive empire. He wrote a couple of books. One of them is the proverbs book. It happened to make it into the *Bible*, but even if you're not religious, read it. A proverb a day. I did this for two years, and it changed my thinking. This is one of the best advantages that I have for getting ahead because proverbs are common-sense, and people say common sense isn't so common, but it's right there in the *Bible*. Again, I know this may sound weird—I'm just telling you this stuff works.

I'm not telling you to read the *Bible*. You can actually go to the bookstore and just get the *Book of Proverbs*. Again, it's not religious stuff. It's practical life stuff. Another good one is Napoleon Hill's *Keys to Success* or *Outwitting the Devil*. But your book that you wake up to should be positive. You can go to the Napoleon Hill Foundation, or you can just Google "Napoleon Hill's Thought for the Day," and get on Napoleon

Hill Foundation's email list. Every day, they'll send you a positive thought affirmation. When I wake up in the morning, the first thing I'm going to do is hit something positive. In this case, it's Joel Osteen's *Become a Better You* book. Now sales books aren't always positive. Business books aren't always positive. I'm not trying to get your mind on business first thing in the morning; I'm trying to get your mind on positivity.

Pick a book that holds back on the cuss words and negativity. You want to open this book before you check out the news for the day. Simply select what will get your mind excited, energized and positive. Put some positivity in your bank account. Maybe you're not into books? That's OK. I suggest you get on somebody's YouTube list and make sure it's somebody who doesn't cuss. Obviously, I'm off that list. So, no cussing and tune into a person who will give you inspiration. Later on, in the day, you can listen to the cussing. It's not a big deal. But the first thing in the morning, I want your mind clear. That's all. You know how breakfast is the most important meal of the day; so, the first bit of knowledge, the first bit of information, that you grab on in the morning is going to be the most important, too. Don't listen to me in traffic screaming at people. The first thing you need is to hit a book or video that's extremely positive. So, that's what I do. And you don't have to read the whole thing or watch an entire movie. I just read a couple of pages. I'm not trying to hurry up through Joel Osteen's book. Each day, I only need a little bit of knowledge to know how I can make a difference with positivity.

If you want to go to YouTube and watch a video, then set yourself up the night before and in the morning, wake up and put your headphones on (if you're next to your significant other). I know I said screens are terrible to look at first thing in the morning, but hey, if you're not going to read a book, we still need to fill your mind with positivity. You don't have to necessarily watch the screen; you could just listen to the audio version of it. Get on Spotify; that's a great resource. Download some old Zig Ziglar motivational audio files, not the sales stuff, the motivational stuff. Go to Nightingale-Conant and download their positive affirmation stuff. You don't want to listen to guys like Garrett J. White and me just for this exercise. Because we will motivate you, but we will also make you angry. You never know exactly what you're getting with us. First thing in the morning, it's important that you hit that positivity account strong. So, I roll over. I read a couple of pages out of Joel Osteen's book; then after I've got my mind right, I read the Thought for the Day on my phone.

After I read the Thought for the Day, I make the decision to get out of bed. Sometimes, I'll pick up another book. Right now, I'm reading a book called *Trust Me, I'm Lying*. After I've gotten my positive vibes then I might switch to *Trust Me, I'm Lying* for a few minutes before I get up because I know this: I have two switches, on and off. As soon as my feet hit the floor outside of that bed, it's game on. I'm not going to stop. I would recommend the same for you.

Positivity. I know that as soon as my feet hit the floor, it's time to get moving. There's no turning back. There's no snooze button. There's no alarm, I've got a mission. It's not about making sales training; it's not about the Saturday or Sunday night killer mentality training; it's about the fact I've got work to do. The same goes for you. It's not about doing mortgages. It's not about handling real estate. You're helping people get in a safe location where they can raise their family to become president or a congressman. They could change the world and be the next John Connor. They could stop the Terminator, for all we know.

You're doing mortgages. You're helping somebody secure a future and a blessing. You're selling insurance, and you're making sure that people are protected in the event a tragedy happens. You're selling cars. You're giving people lifestyle transportation making sure they can gainfully keep their employment. You have to think so much bigger than what it is that you do on the surface. I know that as soon as I hit my feet on the ground, I have to follow that mission. That's how I start my day, and then, I just don't stop moving.

Now, here's how I set some goals. Every night before I go to sleep I have a schedule, and on that schedule, there are a few items I've listed every day that I want to accomplish. I have goals for my team every week, and I have goals for the in-between times that I send out to them, too. I like to call them mandatory goals, and I set the expectation through them. Here's my process

I make a list of everything that needs to be done that week. You know what needs to be done. Let's don't lie to each other. I know what needs to be done on my list, so I make that list. Then I stare at it just like anybody else and think *holy shit, that's a lot of work.* We all do have a lot of stuff to do, and when you write things down on paper, or you put it into Evernote, it shows you that you have that much stuff to do. Then, man, shit gets real. Then what I do, and it sounds cheesy as all get-out, but it works, is I number them. Number those bastards in order of importance. Number one is the number one priority, and usually, for me number 30 means I'll get to it whenever I'm done with the other twenty-nine. When we do manage our list this way, it puts what we need to do in perspective. After everything is numbered, then we know what our most important things to do are.

Follow my buddy Alex Charfen, who's a great guy. Look for "Entrepreneurial Personality Type," his description on Facebook.

I highly recommend joining; just tell him I sent you. Post in the group. He'll let you in it. He's funny. You've got to watch some of his speeches. Anyway, he had us do this exercise that used about 50 pieces of paper, and these were real simple questions demanding one or two-word answers, and I thought *well, how stupid and redundant. I'm above this. I make seven figures a year. I'm not going to do stupid paperwork.* But Alex being the good guy that he is and knowing how to deal with Alpha male personalities like mine, made sure to have me read my answers every damn time. I had to do the exercise, and he knew what he was doing, and I knew what it was he was doing, so I went along with it. At the end, I was extremely relieved that I'd done it because I'd reached some conclusions about myself that I didn't know. My main conclusion being that I need to control my emotions. That's why I'm working on the positivity stuff.

That's why I've been using this routine for a long time now, and I've strayed from it a few times and guess what's happened? More stress has come into my life. Even though I didn't want to do the exercise... I did it, and it improved some areas for me as it expanded my thinking and made me a better person.

I'm suggesting that you do the paperwork I'm giving you, too. The first thing is to put down a list of everything that you need to do and number that shit in order of importance. You know what happens after that, right? You've got to do the stuff. You know what's important. You know what needs to be done, so do what's hard and most important first.

When I work out in the mornings, I run first and then work out because running is the most difficult part. My knees hurt. I'm not exactly a lightweight. I'm running through the hills of these parking garages. It's humid as hell in Texas. I usually have drunk a couple of cocktails the night before—that's how I roll—and running is the hardest part. Lifting weights is easy to me. There's no cardio involved, and cardio kills me.

So, I run first. You see how there's a recurring theme in what I decide to do? Garret J. White said, "I work hard to do hard things." I'll figure it out and push through it and make it happen. That's a recurring theme in every area of my life, and it hasn't always served me well, but when it has served me well it's served me *really* well, So, do the hard stuff first because when you run to the top of the hill, the run down is easy. When I go to the top of the parking garage…let's say it's five floors…it's hard to get to the top. The hills are straight up but running down is easy. If I ran downhill first and got all warmed up that way and then had to hit it uphill that would be way harder. That's the reason that you do the hard stuff first.

When you're setting your goals, and your to-do list, then all of a sudden, you know what your goals are. Goal number one is to knock it out. Goal number two is to knock out the second item. Your goals are to complete what you know you're supposed to do, and that's how you roll. Oftentimes, average people find the easiest task to do first because they might feel: *oh yeah, I have a little list today; I feel good about myself. I'm going to call it cool.* No, you do the hard stuff first because you'll be really thankful that it's over with and behind you. It'll make the next thing that you have to get under your belt that much easier. Here's an analogy: I've already knocked out the biggest dude in the league; this next guy doesn't stand a chance.

That makes a good segue into constant motion.

I said earlier that as soon as my feet hit the floor next to the bed, it's on. It's gym time. It's go time. It's computer time. It's work time. It's book time. As soon as I make the commitment, I'm up. My feet hit the floor. I'm not going to stop. There's a reason I have a shark tattoo on the back of my right leg. I've got one on the back of my arm, too, and I like sharks; don't judge me. They used to call me the Loan Shark as a joke when I did mortgages. But I like sharks, regardless.

A) because they're cool. I mean who doesn't like sharks? If you don't like sharks, you're not cool. The biggest thing about sharks is they don't stop moving. If a shark stops moving, they die. A shark has got to be in constant motion, and I think it has something to do with the air going through their gills. Sharks don't stop moving. If a shark stops moving, it dies. I feel like a shark most days.

If I do stop moving it's almost as if I died. If you asked Amy about family movie night, she would be like, "Ryan is the worst family movie night participant in the history of family movie night participants." Because as soon as you get me still, I go to sleep because I'm not committed anymore. I realize that, shit, I've got so much energy that I produced into the atmosphere around me that when it's gone, and I'm still, it's gone. I'm sleeping. I've got to recoup it. I've got to plug my battery in and charge it. It's constant motion, and maybe you're wondering, *well, how the hell do you have constant motion? I'm tired as it is.* Here are some instructions. You create constant motion. It doesn't just happen. You have to make a conscious decision. When I did mortgages, I was in constant motion. Either I was on the phone making calls, or I was making postcards, or writing campaigns, sending emails, knocking on doors, taking pictures, meeting people, locking loans, whatever I could do. When I sold car washes, if there wasn't a car around, I was picking up trash. I was vacuuming the other cars. I was cleaning the lobby. I was taking the trash out. I was picking up things on a lot. I've even mowed the yard, folded the towels, whatever keeps you moving because when you stop, you get lazy.

What happens is a lot of people have stopped so many times that the stopping has become the norm and they don't even realize that they're getting lazy, but they're not in constant motion. They're at about 30 percent motion. If you've ever seen me at a live event, you'll know that I don't stop. Back and forth, back and forth, back and forth. I'm probably one of the worst. I'm sure my buddy Marshall Sylver would agree with me on this that I'm probably one of the worst public speakers ever. If you watched my presentation, I'm back and forth. The event that I just did at Emerald…back and forth, back and forth. I'm in constant motion. The way to become in constant motion is to make a habit out of constant motion, and honestly, it starts with working out in the morning.

It goes back to doing the hard things first. Fucking working out is hard. You're lying to yourself and me if you don't admit that it is. If you say working out is not hard; it's fun, well, I didn't say it wasn't fun. I said it's hard. As an adult, it's one of the hardest things that we do. Working ain't hard; work is stressful. It ain't hard. Nobody taking in this information right now swings a shovel or a hammer for a living. We're behind a keyboard somewhere, shuffling papers online. Just be real, myself included. Working out is hard, it's one of the hardest things we do as adults, but you need to get that knocked out first. And once you start working out, what are you doing? You're in motion.

While you're in motion, what are you creating? More motion and then you charge yourself up for the day. So, you would think if you woke up early and you worked out first thing in the morning, you'd think you'd be tired the rest of the day, but that's not how it works. The fact that you got the energy levels inside your body up, the fact that you got yourself up moving, makes it easier to push throughout the entire day because you're creating that first process of constant motion. Hey, I'm no saint. I don't work out seven days a week, but I commit to working out a minimum of three days every week. Most weeks, it's four. Sometimes, if I'm on a tear, it's five. When I move to Plano and join another CrossFit gym since I won't have a gym in my building, I'll probably be back to five days a week.

Right now, I do a minimum of three, and I want you to think about doing those workouts first thing in the morning, too, so you can create that constant motion. That's the most energy you're going to put physically toward anything, and that physical energy feeds your mental energy and allows you to continue to produce energy. Constant motion is the key. There are three keys to the high-producer mentality. You need to write these down, as DJ Khaled says, "major key," guys. "Major key" alert over here.

Three keys: faster, bigger and better. A high producer, an energy producer, is always consistently striving to be faster. You can relate that to the gym as well. If you get your workout knocked out faster if you can run that mile faster, that's the whole point, right? Challenge yourself every day. If you can do it faster, if you can make it bigger, if you can scale it, if you can do it better, if you can spend more on it, if you can have some more leads, if you can get more referral partners, if you can help more customers, if you could capture more money, it's better. Always strive for improvement, and this transcends into every area of your life. Now, when I say bigger, better, faster…or faster, bigger, better, whatever order you want to put them in, I'm talking about applying that to every area of your life.

I'm not talking about at work. How you can close faster. How you can sell cars faster. How you can do bigger loans. How you can have a bigger process. That's cool, but what about internally as well? How can I personally get faster? How can I do what used to take me ten hours in nine? How can I do what should take me nine hours in seven? How can I personally be better every day? How can I be a bigger person, not just physically from a workout perspective? Some of you ladies are definitely not trying to get bigger. When ladies work out, they want to get smaller. I mean how can you have a bigger mentality, become a bigger person, and then how can you always strive to become better?

One of the things that helped me out and kept me on track and has helped me to stay a high producer is following a schedule. Ever since I was young, I've been on a schedule. Same with you. You have school, the stuff you did after school, and then the schedule on the weekends. Many of us came from broken homes, so we had schedules with moms, schedules with dads, schedules for the extracurricular as they say in Texas over here…by George Bush. Then, when you become an adult, there's nobody holding you to those schedules anymore, and you just let it go. Sure, you show up at work, but many of us work in an environment where you don't have to be there at a specific time. How you do anything is how you do everything, so you probably know that you should be there at 8:00, or 7:30, or 9:00, or whatever, but you probably show up a little bit later than that because that's just how most people are. I'm not knocking you. I'm just asking you to be self-aware if that's you.

Routines are mandatory, and my routine is this: every night before I go to sleep I check my emails and make sure there are no emails in my inbox. We use Gmail for an email provider. I use Google Inbox, which is an app you can get on both your Android and your iPhone. I have both phones now. I got tired of the Android people shooting me down. But it's an app you can get on both phones, and you can swipe left or right for emails, and it packages them up. It's a totally cool program, and it takes you a couple of minutes to set it up. I can sort through the emails within a matter of minutes and make sure that all emails are replied to. I do the same thing for Facebook messages, Voxer messages from my team and group comments. When I lay it down for the night, I make sure that I have finished and closed my day, Guess what? That allows me to compartmentalize, and that's important, especially as a man because that's what men do. We compartmentalize stuff. It's like *OK, that job is done. Let's move to the next phase.*

At the end of the night, if I've answered every email if I've answered every message, then I'm able to move on. Some of you have email notifications up in the thousands on your phone. I see your screenshots, and you wonder why you stay stressed. Because you can't even get closure on your email inbox, let alone some other areas of your life. Don't shoot me down for telling the truth. That doesn't mean I don't love you. It just means I'm thinking of you. Routines are mandatory. My routine is I make sure all that stuff is done before I go to sleep. At the end of my day, I'm finishing compartmentalizing and closing things down. That allows me to do one of the most important things that you can do as a human... I get good-ass sleep. Think about it. If I don't have stress about waking up to something that I didn't handle that day, I don't have stress when I sleep. I can get four hours of bad-ass good sleep that most can't get in ten.

Do you know why? Because I finish my day, I compartmentalize my exercises; my day is done. There's no more stress. Anything that's going to happen is going to happen in the future. It's out of my control. I might as well go to sleep and enjoy the rest that I'm going to get because as soon as my feet hit the ground in the morning, what's going to happen? Constant motion. Do you see a pattern here? See how it all ties together? This is not a schedule for the weak. There's a reason I'm separated from a lot of other people; it's because I stick to the schedule. This isn't a schedule for the fallen; this is the Bruce Lee of business schedules. It will kick your ass, but it's also the best, in my humble opinion. I finish my day. I get a good four to six hours of sleep. That's all I need because I'm getting real sleep. I believe people who need 10 hours of sleep aren't really sleeping.

I used to watch Amy when she worked for the hedge fund. You know, we sleep in the bed together, obviously. Even when we were splitting time between Scottsdale, I would watch her. You know, she's beautiful. I like to stare at her when she's sleeping anyways because it's like the one time that you can do that. It's not really creepy. She's beautiful. I like to stare at her, but I watched her toss and turn in her sleep back in the day when she worked for the hedge fund. Her day was never finished. The stock market could dip overnight. She was going to wake up to new drama in the morning. She hit the snooze button multiple times in the morning. I shit you not; she would turn the alarm on at 5:30 and she would have a 5:30, a 5:40, a

5:50, a 6:00, the 6:15 and she'd wake up at 6:30 finally. She had all of these alarms set on her phone. Her number one was labeled "Snooze Me." Alarm number two was "Hair and Makeup, 8 Minutes." She had this down. I'm sure they're still in her phone.

The funny thing was she couldn't wake up in the morning because she couldn't sleep. She was in a constant, perpetual state of stress because she didn't compartmentalize and finish her work for the day. The eight hours of sleep she got were really the equivalent of about two hours because her mind was racing since she hadn't put to bed what needed to be put to bed the day before. Many of your minds race about stuff that doesn't even have to do with work. Child support, shit, mine's as expensive as anybody else's. Business deals, whether or not we're going to make payroll. Investments that we put our money into. People suing us. All different things that can happen to you. Stress with the significant other, stress with kids in school, stress with maybe your kids doing drugs, or you not being able to kick your own personal habits.

We all have stress that we deal with, but we just need to compartmentalize it and finish it. Because if you can get a good night's sleep, and then wake up to think about how you're building onto what you just handled, you finish the day. When we do this, we get a good night's sleep. We wake up in the morning, and it's instant positivity.

The next thing is we need to work out, get constant motion going, and then we can tackle the day like fucking Billy Bob Badass. I never met anybody named Billy Bob Badass, but we can just assume that he'd be a bad motherfucker if he existed. He might exist. Google that shit.

I'll give you a couple of hacks that work really well for me in my day.

Like I mentioned, use Google Apps; it's free. Then manage your calendar. I added my Gmail calendar to my phone, Remember that list—order of importance—the 1-30 items? First, all those things are in my calendar. I put them in there. Nine o'clock, number one; ten o'clock, number two, or maybe eleven o'clock, depending on how long nine o'clock's was. I put all of those in my calendar. When I go to sleep at night, I make sure I have clothes ready, and all the other details are taken care of. Then I take a look at everything that's coming in the future, everything I've already gotten written in my calendar. *OK,* I think, *these are things I need to do tomorrow, cool. Did I get everything on my list today? No, oh shit I didn't. Go back and do it, Ryan. You can't go to sleep yet.*

There's never an "I'll get it tomorrow." No, no, no, that's not how we work. The "I'll get it tomorrow" crowd never got shit. Even Garth Brooks will tell you "tomorrow never comes" and a procrastinator is all about "I'll do it tomorrow."

I don't know anybody who has ever procrastinated themselves into high production or ever procrastinated themselves into any winning position whatsoever. Except for that movie, *The Great White Hype* with Damon Wayans and Woody Harrelson, where Damon Wayans procrastinated on working? I'm not going to tell you how it ended but if you've never seen that movie, it's a great one. *The Great White Hype*, good shit. Other than that one Hollywood example, it doesn't exist. Procrastination is bullshit. Get the calendar on your phone and put your list in there. Make sure that you finish the stuff from the day before going to sleep and make yourself aware of what you have to do tomorrow. I make myself aware of what I have to do tomorrow because I know that if I've got a lot of stuff to do, then I need to let my mind know that these next four hours *I have to get some good sleep, Ryan*. I need to be in some serious level five, stage-12 REM sleep because I have to get up early, and I have a full day. I have to have a lot of energy, and I have to produce.

If I know that I have a busy-ass day on tap, then my mind's

going to wake me up at 4:30 a.m. It's not going to wake me up at 6:30 a.m. It's going to wake me up at 4:30 a.m. It's going to go *are you ready to hit the ground, baby? Let's move.* Keep that calendar on your phone. That way you don't have to carry a pen and paper around. You don't have to have the calendar across your desktop. You know my family, and Lindsay and Pat and Roxanne, and every one of my clients gets on my calendar. That's how billionaires work. I'm not a billionaire, just a disclaimer, but that's how billionaires work. You get on their calendar. A calendar dictates their life. If you watch the show *Billions* with Bobby Axelrod, the way that he rolls through their time is, he is on a schedule and time revolves around him. That schedule draws him wherever, but when you're on the calendar, and things are listed for your tasks, it's dictating to you what needs to be done, and it's holding you accountable.

Did you finish the 9:00 task? Oh, you didn't? Well, why are you being a lazy bitch? You can see it right there, and if you look at it and know you didn't do it, then you know subconsciously and consciously, that it's only your fault. Ask yourself this: *Would a high-level producer skip things? If I'm skipping this, what else am I skipping? If I tend to put this off and procrastinate on it, what other areas of my life am I procrastinating in?* Now that I've hopefully made you aware that these things exist and now that you are aware of some of the habits that are holding you back here and some of the habits that are holding you back there, I want you to start becoming aware. Anchor that moment and ask yourself why. When you find yourself coming to an "I'll do it later" statement, stop, anchor it and ask yourself why. *Why do I want to do it later? Why don't I do it now?* Is it because it's hard? Because as I've told you, the hard things need to get done first.

If it's hard and I do it later, then I'm only cheating myself, because I know that it's easier to run downhill than it is uphill. It's simple physics. The calendar is huge, one of the things that I use with my family. Again, my clients get on my schedule. Lindsay needs me; she gets on my schedule. She doesn't just randomly text me unless it's an emergency, which rarely happens, but if we need to talk she looks in my calendar or she adds it to my calendar. My fiancée, soon wife-to-be, beautiful Amy gets on my calendar. She doesn't come to me and say, "Hey, when's the time we can do this?" She has to log into my calendar, and she schedules a meeting. If Jackson and Asher have something they want to do tomorrow, I look at my calendar, and I tell them what time we can do it. I don't just say, "...if we get to it," but when I put it on my calendar that makes it real to where I show up for my kids. If I put it on my calendar and I know that by 6:00 I have to take Asher and Jackson to the jump park, so they can burn some energy, also so they get their version of REM sleep, and it's on my calendar, there's no excuse. It holds me accountable.

We'll write our whole business schedule out, but we won't schedule time for our kids. You might say, "What kind of a weird dude has his wife and kids schedule time with them?" One that cares enough about my wife and kids to make sure they're on my schedule. Because here's what I know, if we can all get on the same page no matter what page it is, we can all go where we want to go on that page. First, I fought resistance. I fought resistance with my ex-wife. She felt like she was above scheduling time on my calendar; we're not together anymore. That was a sign of how she showed up at one place in my life, and I'm not knocking her, I'm just saying I had to get Amy and the kids on board, too. It wasn't like, "Oh, OK sure, what time on your schedule?" I felt like a fucking punk, but whatever. I'm sure she had that awkward feeling, but I explained this is how it works. But if you're on the schedule, that means you're important because that schedule is important, so that means I will take the time for you, and I will make sure that you get my attention during that time.

If it's not on the schedule, I can't assure you of anything. Same with Jackson and Asher. "We're not going now, but I've put it on the schedule for tomorrow at six o'clock. I'll let you know when that is, but just know that we're going." Guess what else that saves me? The "When are we going to do this, Dad?" The "When are we going to do this, Ryan?" It's on the fucking schedule. Look it up. It makes it real. One of the tools that I use for them and my clients and everything else in my life is MeetMe. Or, you can go to ScheduleOnce.com. MeetMe is about 20 bucks a month, maybe 30 on the high side. I don't remember because it's auto-billed every month, but it's affordable. I just give anybody my link.

If somebody is like, "Hey, man I'd like to talk to you about XYZ." Boom! Here's my MeetMe calendar because if you're important, you're on my calendar and you have the link to it. It's up to you to pick a time. I'm not going to waste time going back and forth again just like Steve Jobs didn't waste time on what clothes he was going to wear each day. I'm not going to waste time on when your calendar is open and when mine's open. Instead, I'll efficiently send you a link and let you find a position that is open for me. A lot of my well-to-do friends use the same or a similar type of system. Because again, anything that you can do to cut corners and save time when you're a high producer allows you to go back into production. The last part of this section about following a schedule is when you have a schedule on your calendar every day you can measure results.

Did I do this? How many of these tasks did I do? Did I tackle these in order of importance? Did I put this off? Why did I put this off? Did I do more stuff this month than I did last month?

Guess what? It's all tracked. How cool is that? I'm not worried about an alibi; every freaking hour of my life pretty much is documented in Google calendars. As my kids go back, maybe future publishers or whatever the case may be, as they go back they'll be able to look, and they'll say, "This guy did all of this stuff. Look, he used to do like hardly anything and then look, over the years, he jam-packed all this stuff into his schedule because he figured out how to really turn this high-production thing up a level or two." I can go back and look at last month and see that I entered 400 different accounts into my calendar and this month I can see that I made more money and I put 500 in. Better, bigger, faster. See the recurring theme here?

When I was at Charfen's place, he explained again, about entrepreneurial momentum. It's funny because I have wanted to share my thoughts on that topic. Momentum is huge. Alex is quite a bit more articulate than I am about this topic because this is his life's work. He says we entrepreneurs tend to fold under high pressure and noise. A good example that he uses is when you're driving down the street, and you're looking for the street that you turn on, do you have to turn the radio down to be able to find it? Sometimes you just need to remove the noise and pressure from your life so that you can perform.

Alex's whole deal is that when you remove the noise and pressure from your life, it allows you to spend into momentum. Momentum is a word that I use as well with my sales team often because I believe that's what we are in right now. There are two levels again, and Adam Stark is the one that coined this, and I straight take it from him because I love it and will use it at Break Free Academy. But there are two levels of entrepreneurialism. There's the hustle level, which we all have to go through. See, if you skip the hustle level, you never get to level two. Let me give you an example of the hustle level. When I created HardcoreCloser.com, I had to hustle to get 300-400 blog posts on there over the years. I had to hustle to get all of those videos up. I had to hustle to put it together. I had to hustle to build the site myself. I made the logo with software called Gimp. It looked like shit. The whole site looked like shit, and it loaded like shit. It was a terrible site, but I was hustling, and I made it happen. Some people are on limited budgets for their real estate business. Some are on limited budgets for whatever business they might be in, and they need to hustle.

You cannot skip that phase because of two things: When you skip that phase you're not respected. *Oh, he got money from his daddy. Oh, he just has this shit handed to him.* When you skip that phase, you're not respected, but you don't get the experience either. It's not 10,000 hours that makes you an expert. It's that you've gained the experience to become an expert. If you skip the hustle mode, you can't go to level two, because you didn't complete level one. It's almost as if you procrastinated again and said, "I'll get to that tomorrow." Just know there is a light at the end of the tunnel from hustle mode.

I spent last night at Kevin Nation's house. If you don't know Kevin, he's an amazing guy. I'm so blessed to call him my friend and I don't say that about hardly anybody in all reality.

Kevin is just a magnificent, special human being. He really is. My homie, AJ Roberts was over there, too. It was really cool to run into him and his new fiancée Jamie. They've been together forever, and they're about to get married. That's really awesome.

It was great to spend time with him, and Kevin is in phase two. Phase two is highly-paid mode, and you can get there from hustle mode. That's why I had to put in all the work to get Hardcore Closer to where it is, but I had to shift out of hustle mode to go into highly-paid mode. Because listen, high-paid people and hustlers aren't the same.

When I hustled, I made decent money, $20,000-30,000 a month gross income for bills and expenses and stuff. I got to keep a little bit of it, but once I went through the experiments and the experience to become an expert, went through all the hustle, I shifted my mindset to highly-paid. Now, we pull in $150,000 a month on the regular; $150,000 is a slow month for me, and I'm not out there hustling every day. Sure, I've been on the road the last three weeks. But last year, I hardly went on the road at all. Sure, I've got a schedule where as soon as my feet hit the ground I'm constantly moving, but I'm doing the high-level things that are going to get me paid. For example, for me, I'm not actually doing the small stuff anymore. When I write a blog post, I write in Evernote, and I hand that link over to my editor. I write the rough draft, all about 1,200 words. She makes sure that it's been spellchecked; she makes sure that it makes sense because I write like a freaking fourth grader sometimes because I get in a hurry, imagine that. She makes sure that the right pictures are there from our picture account. She makes sure that the right hyperlinks are there. She makes sure that the right SEO stuff is done for it.

Those are things that I had to do in hustler mode, but now I'm in high-pay mode. Why the fuck would I be spending my time doing that shit? I'm not knocking Hilary for doing that stuff; that's her job. As a CEO of a company, that's something that a hustler does. Once I finished that phase, I had to go into high-paid mode. When I was in hustle mode, I answered questions from the sales team. Now that I'm in high-pay mode, I've got Roxanne handling that. Doing all the tech stuff and building the funnels. When I was in hustle mode, that's what I did. Now that I'm in high-pay mode, that's what other people do. I'm not by any stretch of the imagination knocking anybody who does these jobs for my corporation, but what I'm saying is I've had to elevate my thinking to elevate my life. You might be in that state right now—you can't skip it. If you do, you don't gain the experience. But there is a time when you can move ahead. The voice will tell you when you have to make that shift.

You can't have one without the other, but you have to have

that shift. The reason I tell you that is that hustling is what leads to momentum.

Back in 2008; I was released from federal prison and helped build a nice Church in Frisco. I refinanced a lot of people there, and they gave their money to the church, so they could build it. When I got out of prison, I thought these guys were good friends. I thought they were people who were looking out for me because I was a dude who was a good guy who'd just gotten out of prison and who'd been dealt bad cards. Well, it turns out they invited me to a multi-level marketing event. *Whatever, I'll check it out. These guys are really nice to me.* It's not like they visited me in prison or anything like that and looking back, they were taking advantage of me in a vulnerable position...that I wasn't in, but I was open-minded enough to check it out. And these guys said they were making a little money, so that was cool.

I remember Steven K. Scott. He was a billionaire who invented the Total Gym. The Chuck Norris, Christie Brinkley ads, that's his product. He owned the company, and he said, "We are at the tipping point of momentum," and I'd never heard that phrase before. They explained the hustle to high-pay role right there for the first time. They were showing that in their first year, they got 50,000 people on board, the second year they had 250K and so on (or whatever their numbers were). They were showing the chart where in the last year there had been 800,000 people on board. And 854,000 has been the traditional tipping point for how multi-level marketing companies work. So, I knew that meant they were about to be in momentum. They said momentum makes the chart go from a slow crawl to a steep incline. When you look at momentum on the chart, there's a sharp spike for the day, for the week, for the year. Because when you think about it, Apple stock and Google stock have gone up to $700 and $1,000 and then had to split 5 to 10 times to make it affordable again. There was a point when Apple stock just went straight up; the same thing happened with gas stocks a few years ago.

Kind of like back in the day when mortgage stocks went all the way down. This is just the opposite. It's not a pyramid; it's a pizza. In order to hit that momentum, you're not going to get there by accident. They didn't get there organically. No, 20,000 people turned into 800,000, which led these speakers to extremely highly paid positions. These guys that were speaking had gotten out there on the front lines and done this stuff, too. Momentum is important because it's a driving force behind our success; we've got to have something propelling us. We've got to have something we're looking for. That's why the goals I went over earlier are so important. That way, you are using this momentum to accomplish those goals. It's one of the ways that I've been able to stay in momentum in my business for the last two years, now (because anything before that doesn't really matter). It all relates back to staying in constant motion. As soon as my feet hit the ground. I made sure that I didn't stop moving.

You might say *that's a lot of work. That's a big promise. I got to take a break every now and then.* Average people take breaks. Extraordinary people take all they can get. Tweet that if you love it. "Average people take breaks. Extraordinary people take all they can get." I'd like to believe everybody accessing this information is an extraordinary individual. Even if you don't feel like one, I'd like to believe you want to be one. But if you do you're going to have to do things differently than everybody else. You're going to have to do things better than everybody else. You're going to have to do things faster than everybody else. You're going to have to do things on a bigger level than everybody else. Like Donald Trump says, you're going to have to do things "bigly." One of the keys to staying in constant motion is getting blockers on your team. The way the running back stays in constant motion and is able to move his feet the whole time he has the ball is if he's got the right blockers in front of him.

If the running back's going to get to the end zone, somebody's got to block for him. Somebody's got to make sure that he stays in momentum. My blockers are Kevin Nations, AJ Roberts, Lindsay, Amy, Russell Brunson, Garrett J. White, Pat, and Roxanne and several others that I have surrounded myself with. If I have left you out, don't feel bad. I could have gone on with the list forever. When it's my turn to play the right position, I block for them because I've got momentum in my life, too. You have to surround yourself. The Sales Talk With Sales Pro group, and the Own It Academy group are great places to start, but oftentimes, you think you've got yourself surrounded by some blockers, but it's a fucking defense. They're blocking for the other team. They're coming for you, motherfucker. They're not on your side. You've got to surround yourself with extraordinary people if you're going to be an extraordinary person. You've got to get around people better than you who are lifting you up, and you've got to get around people who you are better than so that you can lift them up. You've got to be a blocker, and you've got to have people blocking for you.

Oftentimes, many people play dual roles. You will be blocking and getting blocked for. When I say better, I don't mean that you're a better person than somebody else, but let's just use this logic. If we're all created equal, and I know that I can't jump for shit, and somebody is better than me at jumping, well maybe that person who's better than me at jumping is not better at coming back at sales rejections, right? Because I'm the champion of that shit. When I say better, it's because they're better at specific parts than you are. I may be better at picking up women than Kevin is, maybe not, I don't know. He is better at being an extraordinary person with high-level thinking. I might be better at creating content than Amy, but she's extraordinary at blocking off things that I don't need to bring me down. I've put Amy, Lindsay, Roxanne and Pat in charge of blocking negativity for me. People that comment on my post, drama that starts on the group, people that are hating on me, they keep me away from all that. Why? Because I'm trying to keep this positive account filled over here.

They're blocking for me; they're better at that than I am. Amy and Lindsay can way better handle somebody who's hating because they're not as emotionally attached to it as I am. Both of those ladies have an extreme amount of respect for me, and we have a relationship. It's business that matters to them just as much as it does to me, but at the same time, they are not the person that's being attacked, and they are better to handle it. They're blocking for me. Meanwhile, I'm creating content, running this company, making sure that they get paid, and that they're taken care of. I'm blocking for them. Kevin Nations has a lot more money than me, a bigger real estate portfolio, and a lot more life experiences just because he's an amazing person. He's blocking for me. I'm better at Facebook ads than he is. I'm helping him out. I'm blocking for him. Marshall Sylver's got his life together more than I do; a $220 million net worth, private jets, two mansions, $100,000 watches, fleets of Rolls-Royces, he's living the life. He's got that speaking thing down better than I do. He's blocking for me, bringing me up. Meanwhile, I run Facebook ads better than he does. I'm blocking for him, lifting him up.

You have to surround yourself with amazing people. Now, what if I was hanging out with my Uncle Brian still, the greeter at Wal-Mart? That's what I was surrounded with. Pat's going to hate this, but fuck it, it needs to be said. This is what I told Pat, who's living over here in a condo that's paid off.

Congratulations, at 28-years-old, he's got a paid-off house; how many of you can say that shit? He's had the paid-off house for quite a while. He has practically zero debt, but he's living in a $20,000 or $30,000 condo, and I hear Pat complain to me about the type of people that he's surrounded himself with, (but this was a while back). I said, "Man, you can't hang out over there and expect to get over here, where we're at in this penthouse. You are surrounding yourself with different mentality-type of people, and honestly, the type of people that live in this building are never going to go into your neighborhood, so you're not going to find them there." I live in this particular building because of the caliber of people that are here. The people I work out in the gym with are rich. The people that I see in the mail room are rich.

I want to surround myself with amazing people, and you can't do that in the wrong neighborhoods. I understand everybody's limited on funds, but here's what I said to Pat the other day, "Set a goal to get your ass out of there. Paid-off house or not, you can always fall back on that and rent it, but you need to go get yourself somewhere nice to rent and surround yourself with people that are being successful." Shit, Pat's neighbors over there at his old place didn't do anything but peek out the window wondering what he's up to. Now where he's at everybody has a job. So, does Pat now. His life's improving, maybe he's a little bit more stressed out because he's got bills now and he's not used to having to pay for a house. But at the same time, he's removed himself from a situation where he was surrounded by people who weren't going to block for him, and now he's been put in a place that at least, people know what it's like to be blocked for. At least, he can see people getting blocked for. At least, he can see the successful cars that show up there; he can run into the neighbors.

You think it doesn't motivate me to go and see Elgin's Lamborghini, his Bentley, and his McLaren sitting down there every day? He doesn't know it, but he's blocking for me. If you're going to stay in constant motion, you're going to have to surround yourself with momentous people, with amazing folks. Here's the other thing that many struggle with, myself included. I just want to put out there that I am preaching to the choir. You have to burn excess energy. If you're an energy producer and you're producing more than you're demanding, oftentimes, you've got excess energy that you have to burn off because if you don't, it will turn into negative energy. Some of you taking this in are saying, "Son of a bitch, I'm sitting here thinking I don't produce enough. Now, he's teaching me how to get rid of it if I produce too much." If you'll follow my schedule, you'll end up producing too much. It will happen. It's designed that way. If you follow my plan and you may have to read it two or three times, that's OK, but you will have excess energy, and you have to burn that energy. Oftentimes, we get out of shape; we get a stomach on us—guys, we get a stomach—ladies weight tends to go to their thighs and ass, right? Luckily these days, thighs and ass are the big deal.

That's what every guy is looking at. Girls are getting lucky, but nobody's really staring at dudes' bellies right now. We're all self-conscious in one way or another, but things get stored where we don't want them to get stored, that's what I'm saying when it comes to your body. Energy will get stored in places where you don't want it to get stored as well. Cortisol and things of that nature, so you've got to burn it, that's why the gym is so important. Anytime that I've found myself in a situation where I'm fighting with Amy, or in a fight with Lindsay, or I'm mad at the kids, or I'm yelling at contractors, or I'm stressed it's like, "Dude, I've got excess energy I'm going to burn off." Thirty minutes to an hour in the gym, I'm back to normal again. Almost like that Joe Pesci Snickers commercial. You've got to burn that energy off. Working out is crucial. I'm not here to tell you to eat clean and change your life. You should, there's nothing wrong with that, but hey, I like a good Whataburger as much as anybody else. I like good old Texas BBQ, and I am, by no means, in the best shape on the planet, and I'm not here to be a physical trainer.

I make sure I eat good food every chance that I can. Yesterday, we were at the SLS. We rented a cabana there in Vegas, and we could have ordered French fries or anything else, but we ordered a fruit platter because I know that we're going to need energy out there in that hot sun all day and we're going to need to be hydrated. Instead of us eating a bunch of French fries and getting all greasy and being low energy while there's this huge party going on that's obviously going to demand a lot of energy from us, then we need to be eating fruit. That's what we did. We had this huge plate of fruit that we all tackled. It would have been easy for everybody to get hamburgers and be all fat and farting in the pool and everything else. Let's just be real, that's what happens because your body is burning off that extra energy somehow. It's like, dude, we got all this useless negative energy over here, let's just fart it out. Sounds gross, but that's what's going on.

Instead, we have fruit, and I didn't wake up with a hangover this morning. Partly because I spent the wee hours of the night over at Kevin's house and he's not a drinker, and so I just drank water the entire time I was there to make up for the bottle of Grey Goose I drank during the day. When it comes to eating clean foods, here's how I run my day. I eat the biggest and most important meal in the morning. I get that first meal knocked out. I've always followed this: Eat breakfast like a king, lunch like a prince and dinner like a pauper. Because I'm going to have constant momentum, constant motion; then I'm going to eat a big breakfast to fill me up. I know that if I'm going to have constant motion all day, I can't get full again and slow down. I'm going to burn that energy all day from that first big meal, but if I have a big meal at the end of the day, what happens?

When I go to sleep a couple of hours later, not 12 hours later like breakfast, I'm going to have a lot of food and energy left over in my body. It's going to cause me to have excess weight. It's going to take more energy to move that excess weight, and it's going to be that much harder, dammit, to be able to get into momentum. Because how you do anything is how you do everything. You see how this correlates all the way back from the start? Clean energy is huge, good foods, all of those decisions, are very important.

You need to find mentors, blockers. Kevin's obviously, a mentor of mine, Russell Brunson is a mentor, and I've had dozens upon dozens of them over the years, but you need to find a mentor. I can't explain how being in these mastermind programs has changed my life. See, I had never heard of masterminds. I'd never heard of anything about them, but it sounded so awesome that Carnegie and those guys surrounded themselves with all of these other smart, brilliant people. I wondered *where the fuck am I going to find people like that*? I went to church. That's a natural, logical thing to do, especially coming in here from the South because I wanted to surround myself with other like-minded people.

Then I became friends with and found my first mentor through a church home group. I was introduced to the whole

Internet marketing thing, and they have masterminds like business people do, and I wasn't interested in masterminding with people about the church. I put up with the church stuff, so I could ask my mentor, Rick Jones about business stuff. "Hey man, how did you get these storage facilities? Because that's my goal, I want to raise money to be the largest car wash chain in America. I want to be a guy that owns multiple apartment complexes. I want to have a huge Internet portfolio. This Internet marketing thing, it's just the beginning for me." I've had to start all over. This is how I started building my empire so much bigger than what's in front of me right now. I've known this for years. I just haven't had the means to be able to do it until recently, but Rick Jones is somebody who had done it. He owns Advantage Storage. They're a huge chain here in Texas. We went to that church, and I endured all the "Father, Lord in heaven" that I didn't care that much about in order to get close to him for business because I knew that was the only way I was going to find a mentor.

I knew that was the only way I was going to be in any kind of mastermind because, much like you, I didn't go to MIT. I don't have a Harvard degree. I wasn't even allowed at the college of the community. Where was I going to find a mastermind? I obviously, got involved with Frank Kern, and he had a mastermind, and it was an 8-week program alongside a gentleman named Kevin Nations for $8,000. That would be a steal from them if you could find it now. See, that's why you become an early adopter right there.

When I was with Kevin, I paid $20,000. That was just a couple of years ago. Now, that same thing costs $70,000 and, of course, it's evolved a lot over the last couple of years, but I wouldn't be able to afford that these days. Even still now, that's a lot of money. But back then being an early adopter, I got all the benefits at a steeply discounted price. I want you to think with that mentality, too.

A gentleman was going to join my Tribe, and The Tribe was $12,500 for six months. That's where you work personally with me. You have my phone number. We talk as much or as little as you want. You can access the people in the group—several of them are millionaires back there as well. Smart people doing great things. You have our meet-ups, come to Break Free Academy. It's a hell of a deal for 12, five, or six months and most people end up lasting longer. But he procrastinated. He called four or five Tribe members and asked them about it, and it's not like anybody who's a paying customer is going to say anything bad about me. Go ask a hater if you want to hear anything bad about me. If you're looking for negative testimonials, you're not going to be somebody I'm getting money from right now. The only negative testimonials I have for the record, are from people who are kangaroos, who have screwed me over at one point or another. I bet you, anybody who gave negative testimony I have them somewhere saying some positive stuff on video. That's just how it works.

But this guy waits about three weeks, said he's in, and talks to a bunch of people then waits some more. Then he hit me up the other day, and I told him, "Hey man, well, we raised the price to 30 grand for 12 months. I've been wanting to do that for a while. I thought that 24 grand for 12 months was cool, but I really don't want to just work with somebody for six months. I want to work with somebody for years, and I believe that the type of person that I'm trying to attract and work with, want to work with me for years as well. And I believe that the relationship that we're building and our track record of helping people is worth way more than just the $24,000 a year and the fact of me having to resell you again potentially, in six months. I'd rather just have a year contract that's moving forward. We renew it again next year. Makes it that much easier because, in a year's time, there's no doubt in my mind whatsoever, that you'll have made your money back and a significant amount more. Many people have made more than their full investment back in a month. Because of the caliber of people that I attract." That's the reason I say that being an early adopter will help you. I took Warrior for $20,000; I think Warrior is $40,000 now, too.

If you get the opportunity to be in a mastermind, make sure you're in a mastermind full of people that are higher level. The last thing you want to do is be the smartest dude in the mastermind. The last thing that you want to do is be *the* mastermind. You want to plug into a group of people that can lift you up, a group of people that can block for you. Plus, if you're smart, you'll network with the people in the mastermind and figure out additional ways to make money. You don't just make money from the guy that's leading the mastermind; you make money from it. I paid eight grand to Kevin and Frank, and it changed my life. Since then, I've joined Warrior; I've joined Russell, Brian Horn, Donald Wilson, you name it, I've been in their stuff over the years. With some of these guys, I've made more money than ever before. I'm better than all of them except for maybe Kevin at sales. I'd give Kevin a damn run for his money. I joined with these guys because there was some area or another where they were better than me.

There are some guys in my Tribe that make more money than I do. James, David, Jim…they probably all make more money than I do. It's not even corporate money. Obviously, I have a mastermind. We call it The Tribe.

You've got to surround yourself with people who can block for you. Being in masterminds has changed my life. It's put me in momentum. Even when I went to Boise, Idaho.

Take, for example, Lindsay. She's not in sales, and neither is Pat. They were just up there with me and to even watch those two go in the room and see how a mastermind works together, well, they got excited. Lindsay came home with 10 pages of notes. Pat came home with a full binder of notes, ideas that came to their minds outside of things that I thought of at this mastermind. Because we surround ourselves with a bunch of smart people.

I just want to encourage you. I just want you to consider that there are big things for each and every one of you, or you wouldn't absorb this content. If you don't align yourself with the right people at the right time and the right place, the right things won't happen for you. I believe that when you get into a state of momentum, and you're in hustle mode, then when you surround yourself with other people in hustle mode, who are also in a state of momentum, that great things will happen.

I have experienced it several times in my life, and I'd like to encourage you to experience it in your life, and obviously, I want to be the person to lead that experience for you. But in the event that is not me, find someone. In the event that it's not me, hire Russell, or Kevin, or somebody mentioned before. Hire someone's who's been there, done that, and that you know can tell you from experience what you should consider. They're not extracting information from someone else's experience. Because masterminds do matter.

Here's your homework, or what you need to follow up with after you finish this chapter. Whatever time you normally wake up, wake up an hour earlier. Don't make an excuse. I don't have any way of tracking or verifying it. You have to be accountable to yourself, so just don't be a lazy bitch. It's that simple, one hour earlier every day this week. It's not that hard. What's one hour? You'll compartmentalize your day, and you'll finish strong, then you'll get that REM sleep, and it won't ever be missed.

Step number two is to exercise three times this week. Number one, wake up an hour earlier every day this week for the next seven days. Number two, exercise at least three times this week. If you already exercise, add some minutes to your time.

Number three, only be still when you sleep. Constant momentum this weekend is the goal. One week, just follow what I'm telling you for one week, and it will change your lives. Last, but not least, create a schedule and follow it. I told you, don't be a lazy bitch. Quit shorting areas of your life. It's not serving you well. Create the schedule; only be still when you sleep; exercise at least three times this week and wake up an hour earlier every day. You won't miss the sleep, and if you follow the schedule and close the schedule every night, you'll sleep better, and that hour will not be missed. You will actually wake up with an extra hour in your day to be a high producer without being tired.

It's fucking crazy, but it works, I promise. I'm living proof. I believe that each and every person who has taken the time to learn about these methods can be a high producer. You have the capacity to be a creator on a larger level than where you are at right now, whether you're creating content or whatever your contribution is. I want you to finish this chapter with a different mentality, the high-producer's mentality. Read this chapter more than once. Live what you've read. More importantly and finally, show up in every single area of your life in the best way that you can with the highest production and the most momentum possible for you.

Do these four things this week: Wake up an hour earlier; exercise three times; only be still when you sleep and create your schedule and follow it. Compartmentalizing, getting sleep, that will change your life.

Chapter #3: Dealing with Your Demons

Own It Academy is the title of the group we have on Facebook and the lessons I am expanding upon in this book. The name fits because this book's about owning your bullshit and moving forward.

That's one of the reasons I've been able to build my successful sales training business. I don't fuck around. I'm not playing gimmicks. I'm being straight-up.

In this chapter, we're going to have to get real with ourselves. I'm going to get real with you, and I'm going to tell you some shit that I really haven't shared with very many people. You have to ask yourself if what I'm saying resonates with you or not because here's the thing. Every word that you read, your brain is processing that for three words and what I'm saying is your brain is thinking three or more ways through it to see if it agrees with me or not. So, for every word, your brain's doing three times the work, processing three times the words because it's putting angles on it.

Do I agree with this guy? Is what he's saying right? Is this bullshit? So, I need you to get real, and I need you to make a decision to be all here. You've made the time.

We're really going to look inside of ourselves, the part where we start to figure out where all this shit came from. The part where you learn my process for overcoming this shit. I've been through a lot of shit. It's not like I have fucking life together over here. I'm not sitting in front of you going, "I have it all. I have this fucking perfect life." No, fuck, I do not, but I'm telling you, I've had a fucked-up life that I've made the most with, right? Life's thrown a lot of lemons at me.

I live down the street from a liquor store, so I made vodka lemonade, and I'm going to share with you how I've been able to do this because a lot of the things that I've dealt with (I'm going to be the opposite of humble here) would've killed a bunch of motherfuckers. They would've killed themselves; they would've gotten killed in that situation; they would have had heart attacks. They just wouldn't have made it, and I'm not saying that I'm tougher than most or tougher than many, but I'm saying I've survived this shit and the things that I'm going to share with you, I've come out on the other side, survived through these things. And you have to make a decision as you learn this process whether it's going to fucking work for you or not, whether you believe me or whether it's bullshit or whether it's hokey. And all I ask is to just for the sake of everything, just fucking pretend that I'm right. Even if your brain tells you that I'm wrong, just fucking pretend that I'm right, because what if I am, and what if the shit that you learn that I'm about to drop on you, changes the course of your life? What if it changes your destiny; it awakens that voice in the back of your head; it steers you on the path? Just what if I'm fucking right?

I can promise you this. Whatever your brain tells you when it's making those three decisions for every word that you take in, remember this: It'd be a lot cooler if I was right and we can fix this shit than if I'm completely fucking wrong and we just stay where we're at right now. I'd rather be right, and I hope that you trust me to be right as well.

All right, so let's dig in here.

We're going to deal with your demons. We all have them. We're addicted to all sorts of fucking weird shit, and really, it's not weird, right? We think it's weird, but if we actually talk about the weird shit, we find out it's not that weird, and there's more on that later. That's like a fucking Fox News segment, isn't it? "More on that later."

We have demons. Drugs, lies, childhood issues, you have all these things that you've never dealt with. We spend our whole fucking lives running. We spend our life channeling these things that we need to face and confront. It's like, we know we can just step up and punch that motherfucking bully in its motherfucking mouth until he quits talking shit to us and taking our lunchbox, but instead, we try to outrun him every day, knowing that he's going to catch us. Well, let's confront some demons, and move past them.

I'll be the first to tell you; I smoke marijuana every day. I have for, fuck, I don't know how many years because I have short-term-memory effect from smoking marijuana every day. I share that A) because it's hilarious to some people and B) I'm just being real with you. I'm not perfect. I go out drinking, and we have Break Free Academy here on Friday night. We'll all go out to the club, and I'll probably have a $5,000 bar tab because there'll be 30 people drinking. It's not because I'm out of control drinking that much. I'll have some drinks. And sometimes I get fucked; sometimes I don't, and I'm OK with that. I'm not ashamed of that. I don't wake up the next morning feeling ashamed. I wake up the next morning feeling grateful that I hung out with people.

When I was in Las Vegas last weekend, we partied at the Cabana. We got fucked up out in the Cabana. I didn't wake up the next day with regrets, feeling bad that I had gotten fucked up. I woke up the next day thinking, *man, it was awesome that I hung out with my friends and enjoyed a moment with them*, and when you have that mind shift, and you operate with that mental toughness, it changes the game for you. When you get rid of the guilt, and I've already addressed not giving a fuck; this is just going to compound on that, that's got to be part of these demons.

Oftentimes, we're running from demons that don't even have anything to really do with us. They're our parents' demons, or they're our grandparents' demons, or they're fucking somebody else's, our spouse's problem maybe. And here we are, running from their problem when if you would just stop, pivot and turn the fuck around, and punch it in the nose, it would quit bullying you around. So, let's dig deep with these demons. It all starts now. That's where things stem from.

The reason why somebody grows up to be a porn star is because they had daddy issues when they were young, right? The reason why someone grows up and tries heroin is because something didn't go right in their home life. The reason why someone grows up and becomes a Satanist is because something went wrong in the fucking church. Everything stems from something. The reason some guy grows up and goes to jail or goes to prison is because something fucking wasn't right early on. So, I'm going to use myself as an example. My biggest problem, and it's an asset, too, but my biggest problem, is that I can just turn my back on motherfuckers, and I've gotten really good at that.

People in the sales pro group, have all seen me several times where I'm just like, "Fuck that motherfucker. We'd be cool but fuck them. Now we're like big apart."

I know that I let my emotions get the best of me. I go into attack mode fast as a motherfucker, and it's not because I'm by nature a mean person. I won't name names, but I was chilling with somebody very important the other day, and he said, "You know, Ryan, people tell me that you're a great guy, but here's how they tell me you're a great guy." He says, "They tell me they want to find a reason not to like you but when they meet you, it's impossible," and I knew he was trying to give me some constructive criticism, but I knew exactly what he was saying because that's how I position myself.

I'm in my own lane doing my own shit, but I have some childhood issues that fucking make me act a certain way. You see when I was age 0-5, and if you haven't read my *Hardcore Closer* book, you should because it will help you understand where I'm coming from and it'll inspire you. You can't put it down, I promise. But when I was less than five years old, I lived in this little country house in a town with about 1,500 people, with my mom and dad. My grandpa was a banker, and my other grandpa was an entrepreneur on the side in a glass factory, and life was fucking good.

Both sets of my grandparents, by all definitions, were millionaires. And my dad, my birth father, was the champion cutting horse, whatever the fuck you call that person, in the world. He was the number one person at what he did in the entire world. As a young man, I respected my parents. I was on cloud nine. I remember going to see my grandpa and him giving me $100 bills because he owned a bank. I remember going to Easter egg hunts at my grandpa's, and they fucking had all these Easter eggs with all this money in them, and I got like 300 bucks going through this Easter egg hunt. But then it happened, 1985, 1986, the savings and loans crashed, and my grandfather not only lost all the banking branches that he had, my grandma was in for six months in federal prison for cooking the books, trying to help out the local people so that they didn't lose their money.

She wasn't doing stuff for personal gains. She was trying to make sure that the bank could stay open and the people that had invested millions of their dollars in my grandfather's banking business wouldn't lose their money. He owned five or six branches, and bottom line is, she fucked up. Broke some rules, thought she could pull out of it, but it didn't happen. She ended up going to prison, and it destroyed their relationship. My grandpa cheated on my grandma, and he destroyed that relationship; my mom got caught cheating on my dad, destroyed that relationship. My grandfather on the other side lost the glass factory. And all this happened over a 2-3-year period. I went from being the happiest little dude on the planet, with two fucking rich-ass families, to being the laughing stock of this little 1,500 piece-of-shit town.

My mom got caught cheating with one of the fucking banker guys, and it was all known around the fucking city, and my dad fucking bolted out of there and went to move to Fort Worth. I hardly ever saw him again. I think I went to his house one time after they split up and within two years, let's say 1987, my mom had dated a whole bunch of guys, moved to two or three different towns, couldn't make it, moved back to this little shithole town that we lived in and married this fucking redneck, steroid, weightlifter fucking guy that just never left the town. I felt like "That fucking guy?" You ever see the picture of the dude on the truck with the fucking mullet and shit like that, and he's got the weed hanging out his mouth, like, "That's why I fuck my sister." That's who my mom ended up fucking marrying. It's hard for me to say this shit, but I'm just being real.

This guy's got a mullet and everything, and he don't have two cents about him, and sadly for him, he's been adopted, so he didn't know what it was like to have a family or any of that shit. He was adopted by two weirdos that he had as parents, and it is what it is. I'm no qualified fuck to say that, but my dad gets in a situation where he's trying to win the world championship two years in a row, and he owes a bunch of child support to my mother. And my mother being the manipulative person that she is, tells my dad that, "If you'll give up the adoption rights and let Keith..." (Which is the new redneck that she's married to). "...adopt Ryan, then I'll forgive you your child support, and you'd be removed from his life." My dad being the chicken shit he is, fucking gave me up.

That motherfucker. I look at Jax; I took him to his mom's house today at 1:30 on Father's Day. He's been in my house every day since Wednesday. I picked him up from school Wednesday; he's been in my house every day since then. I'm legally only required to get him Wednesday and every other weekend, but his mother and I get along so well, and I compensate her enough to where I can get my kid whenever the hell I want him because I love him. And when I look at Jax, I get a little emotional. I think *how the fuck could a motherfucker leave something like that?* If you have kids, you think, *how the fuck did my parents do this shit?* If you don't have kids, you might start thinking, *man, what the fuck were my parents thinking?*

The thing is we don't fucking know. Our parents didn't fucking know either. We're way fucking smarter than our parents. Our parents are fucking stupid. They didn't even have fucking

Google back then. Have you ever tried to work with somebody as old as your parents? I've had a few clients, God bless them, I'm not going to name any names, but Jesus fucking Christ, it's not easy. Our fucking parents, they just weren't as smart as we are because they didn't have the technology. Their parents before them definitely weren't as smart. We're advanced.

I think Bill Burr says it best. He's like, "You ask your mom 'where does rain come from?' and Mom goes, 'Oh, Jesus is up in heaven, and he's happy to make it rain,'" or some shit like that, and he's like, "Dude, fuck off. I'm getting on Google. It says right here. There's something called the water cycle, bitch. Have you ever heard of this? The fuck are you lying to me for?" See, that's another thing that I do. I get off on humor when shit starts to get real emotional, right? By the way, that redneck she's married to went on to fucking beat me. That's why I have this fucking 6-inch rod in my hand. He choked me out behind the car wash so hard one time that he busted the capillaries in my eyes.

I used to especially fear my dad when it was rainy outside. The car wash will close because you don't wash cars in the fucking rain. There's always some idiot that pulls in, but for the most part, the car wash closed when it rained, and I used to walk home from school on rainy days praying (I'm not even religious. My parents didn't even go to church), that my fucking stepdad's not home. And at this point, he's not even my stepdad anymore; he's my fucking real dad because of my mom. When they say, "Do you want Keith to adopt you?" Like I'm scared as fuck of this guy. What the fuck am I supposed to say? "No," and then I have to deal with the guy who has resentment because I don't want to fucking be adopted by him my whole life? I am a natural people pleaser. It's one of the reasons I'm such a good salesperson, but they put this on me at seven years old, man, and it fucked me up.

I went from the kid that thought he was going to have the fucking world, to this kid who had seen everything turn in a heartbeat and it did some fucking cold-hearted shit to me, man, even at a young age. I realize it these days. I've sat in prison for three years. I've had a lot of time to think about where the fuck I've fucked up, but it was that moment that I learned that shit can change all of a sudden and don't get attached to anything. And maybe it's time you identify that fucking trigger, too. That trigger moment for me was when my parents split up; my grandparents split up. My grandma went to fucking jail. Everybody was poor; everybody had to move into fucking smaller houses all of a sudden, and I got fucking given up for adoption. All within a two-year period of time.

Now I'm not sitting here to fucking say "poor me" shit because, obviously, I'm not that motherfucker, but what I'm getting is real with you. There's a trigger fucking moment in my life that taught me something. The most impressionable time in your life is before you're 10 years old and it taught me something at that moment. "Easy come, easy go, motherfucker. So, be willing to just turn your back on people as quickly as you've seen things turn here." I learned that shit can go downhill south, and then as I got older, I learned that it would be better for me to make shit go downhill south than for shit to take me south with it. Oftentimes, they call that "self-sabotage." I'd rather be the reason some guy fucked up rather than just run the course, and besides, nothing in my life did ever work out. So, I wanted to make sure that I kept that flawless record.

We fall into that stinking thinking. *This shit ain't for me. I had it once. I lost it. It ain't for me.* Especially as a kid. Well, maybe the same thing happens with relationships. We have some childhood shit happen, and it drags over into our relationships. In my case, again, I'll turn my back on a woman fast as hell. I'm just being honest. I'm divorced three times. Now I will say this, I have never filed for divorce, but I'm really good at running fucking people off. I'm really good at making them fucking think it was their idea because that's what happened to me as a kid.

Another thing that we do is we spend our whole lives trying to make our parents happy. My parents put me up. My dad gave me up. My parents take me with them, and I go to school at age eight, and I have a new fucking last name. I'm in the same town. I have to explain to all these kids why my name is not Ryan Russell McCord anymore and why my name is all of a sudden Ryan Stewman, but I'm the same motherfucker they've known since kindergarten. Then I have to tell everybody my personal business…how my dad, piece of shit, gave me up and left, and how this new dude who I don't even like, now I'm carrying his last name. But we ain't even really related because my dad owes some money or some shit. My mom's impatient because grandpa ain't giving her cash anymore, right?

Then I spend my whole life trying to hide that shit when we moved to another city. I would just act like Keith, the redneck, was really my dad. People would say, "You guys look just alike." I'd be like, "Man, fuck you. I don't look nothing like this motherfucker." I'd go along with it as a kid, like, "Oh yeah, whatever, fuck off," but I spent my whole life trying to pretend to be something else for them. I pretended when I was 18 when my real father reconnected with me, or maybe I was 21? But I started pretending like it just never happened. Like he'd just been gone for fucking 15 years, and I hadn't seen him, and I just acted like nothing happened, right? Pretending, trying to protect him. My parents always acted like I was their kid and then my sister came along, and they acted like they didn't know me, and I did whatever I did to protect them as I got older. And I committed crimes, and I dropped out of school, and I went to prison and all these things that you would fucking expect of a kid who had gone through what I'd gone through at that age. I'm a typical textbook fucking moron here, and as I went through that stuff, I pretended like it didn't happen for my parents' sake. When people would ask my parents, my parents would straight-up lie about how I was doing and I would straight-up lie for them.

Do you realize the last time I went to prison was because I was in a home that I had saved my parents from because they're fucking financial idiots? I had bailed them out of this house that I had bought from them and my stepdad or adopted dad, whatever you want to call him, gave me a fucking pistol that I didn't even fucking want. Then when the police kicked in my door because it was a nice house, looking for drugs and there weren't any, they charged me with the gun, and he wouldn't fucking just tell them it was his. I could've avoided going to prison if he would've just told him it was his, but he pretended like he didn't have nothing to do with it and I didn't even ask him for the fucking gun, and I wasn't even home when they kicked the fucking door in.

I look back now, and I think of all the shit that I went through to please my parents. I remember being out of prison the first time for maybe six months, and my dad asked me to sell a machine gun for him. I put that bitch in my car, went and sold it to this dude that I knew through another guy who ended up being a meth dealer. The safe that he opened to get the money out of was full of methamphetamine and I had that moment like *this is a life fucking sentence if I get fucking caught up in this bullshit. And my punk-ass stepdad, what the fuck am I going out of my way to fucking do favors for this motherfucker?* Guess what? He didn't even fucking pay me on the gun. I didn't get a commission or anything like that. I'm fucking facing life sentences for this motherfucker as favors. Have done time.

If my parents would've fucking helped me put some money together the first time, I would've been able to get a lawyer and probably not have done two years the first time which would've probably changed the way that life turned out. And so, I share this stuff with you. This isn't an "Oh Ryan; he's going to go into this thing about his parents." It's not that. I still get passionate about it, upset about it, but it's not that. These people that we try to please, these things that have happened to us at a young age, man, remember we have a family of choice and a family of origin. Your spouse, your kids, the people that you're with, your work, your industry, the community that you serve, that's your family of choice. That's who you need to focus on.

Those who gave fucking birth to you, if they're not bringing value to your life, man, you have to treat them no different than anything else. Just because they raised you a certain way, you don't owe them shit, and I see so many of my friends say, "Well, I can't do this, that or the other because what if my parents find out?" Man, you're a fucking 45-year-old man. You make a half a million dollars a year. The fuck do you care what your parents think? Because the majority of where shit stems from, the majority of the shit that the baggage, the luggage, the fucking bondage, all the shit that we deal with as adults, stems from, is from back then.

Now, I'm not telling you to go shit on your parents. Maybe it wasn't your parents for you. Maybe it was your high school sweetheart. She broke your heart, and that was the trigger point for you. I don't know; I didn't have that happen to me. Maybe it was authority figures. Or maybe you're like me, and you have problems with all of it. You've had a girl break your heart; you've had fucking problems with authority figures; you have problems with your parents. Maybe you were this great golden boy, total jock, sports; everything was perfect. Maybe you were the cheerleader girl. Everything was perfect, and then you got drunk one night, got a DWI. The shit changed your life, right? Maybe you were supposed to be the smartest kid, go off to college and then one day you got into some bullshit, you got in trouble with the cops, and that trigger point changed your life.

Whether it was a relationship, your parents, whatever the case, you have to identify that trigger point because that's where all that shit stems from. Mine happened when I was young. I remember it was September 1st, 1987 when I got adopted, so that would make me seven. You identify that trigger. You identify what it is that you are struggling with, where that baggage comes from, and now that you have maybe taken a few minutes now, maybe you can think about it. Trace it back, get on Ancestry.com, whatever you have to do because I know, as I'm telling that story, you're making three decisions for every word.

That means you're making 30 decisions for every sentence. You're thinking a lot right now. It probably gets you going pretty hard, and that's OK. That's what we're doing here, but I've got a method for overcoming this bullshit, because the difference between me, motherfuckers, and the rest of my family, is that I'm aware that this shit happened, and I've made so many mistakes that I'm tired of getting punished, and I'm tired of getting beat up, and I'm tired of doing shit the hard way. I'm tired of going to jail, tired of paying fucking tickets, tired of dealing with this and that and the other. And I've lived my life by the fucking book. Yes, I've got a smoking problem. That's it. Other than that, I break zero fucking laws in this country.

I'm going to share with you my CATAPULT method, It's an actual acronym, too. I'm going to go through this whole process with you, so you can start to see how you can identify areas in your past where you can just compartmentalize that shit and move on.

We're going to talk about setbacks. Whoever said life is short is an asshole. Life's the longest fucking thing we're ever going to do on this planet. You will not do anything longer than being alive unless it's being dead. Being dead is the only thing that you'll do longer than when you were alive, and you got one hell of a head start being alive, so whoever said life's short was full of shit. Now, what I'm going to do now is go old-school. I'm going to reframe this on you. What I want you to consider is that life is the longest thing that you're going to do, so that anything that happens while you go through that life is shorter than life. It's temporary. There are always exceptions to the rule, but pretty much everything is temporary in life.

Life is the longest thing that we'll ever do. That means the periods that we go through that are tough are temporary. Three years in prison, I look back, and it seems like just a flash. That was 10 years ago. The last 10 years of my life seemed like just a flash. The last 20 years, fuck, I'm 36 years old. The last 36 years of my life seemed just like a flash. Like it was just temporary like it just happened. Yet, here we are telling people life is short, live it to the fullest. Life is long. Life's a fucking marathon. You have to take care of yourself. You have to take care of your brain. You have to take care of your health. If not, the next thing you know, you look up, you're 36 years old, you're fat; you let yourself go.

I see old friends, exes, old acquaintances, co-workers, and maybe it's been five years since I've seen them, and they look totally different. They've totally let themselves go. They've gotten married. They stopped working out. I've been in that situation before, not where I stopped working out, but I've been married. Somebody stopped exercising and taking care of themselves. People get lazy; people get comfortable, but life is long. I challenge you to think this…that setbacks are short because if we know life is the longest thing that we're going to do, a setback is something that's temporary. A setback's something that's only going to last for a finite period of time because life is only for a finite period of time and you're not going to be set back your entire life.

You've never heard anybody ever say that they've had a lifetime of being set back. No, a setback is something that is fucking two steps back, three steps forward. At least two steps back, one step forward. You're always going to spring back from setbacks.

Setbacks are short. Setbacks are temporary. Setbacks are good for you. I told you I was going to reframe this stuff. Setbacks are good for you. Setbacks are learning experiences.

When the quarterback takes the ball from the center, he takes two, maybe three, sometimes as many as 15 or 20 steps back before he launches that fucking ball forward, down the sidelines, into the hands of a wide receiver and ultimately into the end zone. But if he didn't have those 2-20 steps back to be able to gain that momentum, to be able to get that stress and momentum on his arm, to be able to launch and rocket that thing forward into the hands of a wide receiver and ultimately into the end zone…if he didn't have those steps back, he couldn't have made that touchdown.

If he just stood there and didn't move, made no motion and just rocketed his arm down to the sidelines, there would've not been enough time for the wide receiver to run down the sidelines. There would've not been enough time and enough momentum and enough energy built up for him to use his arm to his full capability. The line would've probably plowed his ass over because the center can't hold up those tackles forever. That's the metaphor for life. You've got to go through setbacks that are good for you. Setbacks are short; life is long. Appreciate the setback. Without the setback, there is no touchdown. This is the reframe.

Let's talk about a CATAPULT. Knowing that life is long, and setbacks are short, you have a different way of thinking. You've got to have some mental toughness if you're going to look at the setback and embrace that shit. My buddy says, "Embrace the suck." If you're going to embrace the suck, you'd have to be mentally tough. Mentally tough doesn't mean that you're smart; it doesn't mean that you're stupid; it doesn't mean that you're aggressive; it doesn't mean that you're mean; it doesn't mean you'd be mean mugging people and it doesn't mean you move shit with your mind. What it means is that you're tough enough to see through whatever it is you're focusing on to the end. You're tough enough to see whatever it is that's happened. You're looking at a bigger picture. You're tough enough to remove the emotion, embrace the struggle and use the emotion to move forward.

I got into detail about momentum. Most people are mentally weak. They're weak-minded motherfuckers. They watch the Kardashians; they watch the news. They see a post on Facebook, "Oh, he shot a fucking lion." Motherfuckers have been shooting lions for years. "Oh, he shot a nightclub." Yes, that's a fucking tragedy. Motherfuckers shoot up nightclubs here in Dallas every fucking weekend. I live right across the street to one, where the fucking guns go off all the damn time. This shit happens. Weak people get caught up in that stuff. Weak people start talking about things that they can't fucking control.

Mentally tough people look at things from a different perspective. They don't look at the perspective to complain. They don't look at the perspective to be a victim. They don't look at the perspective to be a hero. They look at it from the perspective of "Here's where I am. How did I get here and how am I going to get out of it?" Even when you're not in the setback, "Here's where I am. How did I get here and how am I going to move forward?" The mentally weak think like this: *oh shit, oh shit, I'm stuck here. I'm fucked up. I'm such a victim.* Mentally tough people think, *how did I get here? Here's where I am. How can I move forward?* Mentally weak people: *oh shit, how did I get here? I'm such a victim.*

Most people aren't mentally tough. Most people would rather complain and become a victim of their circumstance and use that circumstance and that victim of circumstance to have an excuse for failure because it's easier to not do the work. It's easier to get fat and lazy and not go to the gym than it is to go to the fucking gym. It's easier not to make 100 calls to your leads this week than it is to fucking do the work and go call the leads and close the sales. It's easier to sit behind your desk surfing on fucking Facebook than it is to go out prospecting and fucking make some money. The mentally weak do what's easier, and if you look around and you see what average really is, you realize the world's full of mentally weak people.

Here's where I get caught up. I've only surrounded myself with people who are in this one percent mentality, most of them one percent financially. And I live in this bubble, and I've removed the news from my life, and I've removed the newsfeed on my social media outlets. I post on Facebook, and I leave it alone. I let my team do the work on the backend for that shit now. I don't have time to deal with it. I don't have time to deal with the mentally weak. I'm about to do a video tomorrow, where I'm going to read from people who have said mean shit to me in my emails and all my comments and stuff, so it'll be pretty funny. One guy's like, "Hey, the '80's called, they want your sales tactics back."

That's a mentally weak person to comment with some bullshit on social media, but here I am. I'm going to fucking exhaust time. I'm going to because it's hilarious. I'm up for the content obviously, but I know myself. If it wasn't for my team showing me these things, which I don't see anymore, I know I'll get caught up. I haven't controlled my own email. address for two years. Lindsay is Ryan and hardcorecloserryan@hcselling.com. She handles all that shit for me because I get a bunch of fucking hate emails there and if I read them, I'll get caught up in my fucking emotions. I'm aware. I'm mentally tough. I've removed myself from being put in mentally weak situations.

We forget we have this elite factor where we have all this money and all this knowledge and all these cool people surrounding us, and we take advantage of it. You look around. There's a bunch of average fucking people. Look at your family. It's probably full of a bunch of average people. If not your family, look at your office. It's probably full of average people. Look at the management in the company you work for. It's probably full of a bunch of fucking average people. Maybe you're fucking average. I doubt it, but maybe. Maybe this is the kick that you need to get the fuck into above average. Maybe that's why you're here. The world's full of fucking average and below average people, man. The last thing we fucking need is another one. The world needs mentally tough people.

If there were more mentally tough people like us, the mentally weak people would have to toughen up. It would be the cool thing to do. But let's get into these setbacks. The mentally tough look at these setbacks from a different perspective.

When I'm in a setback, I don't look at it like, *oh, here I am. I'm the victim.* Instead, I think, *here's where I am. How did I get here? How can I move forward? Here's where I am. How did I get here? How can I move forward? Oh shit, I'm in a slump. OK, OK, I'm in a slump. All right. I got here because I fucked off the last two weeks. I did go on vacation. Shit, I haven't been making calls. I haven't been plugged into this, that and the other. Jesus Christ, I got a lot of things going. OK, so here's what I'm doing. First, I'm going to knock this out, and then I'm going to do this and this and by this time, I should have this order coming over here.*

Start looking at things like, *oh, OK, so I'm aware of my surroundings. How am I going to crawl out of this hole?* I'm going to give you my CATAPULT method. I think you'll love it. It's going to be huge. My CATAPULT method walks you through the process that I use to escape setbacks. And I'll explain the reason why I use a catapult. Let's take the good old trebuchet model. You've got four wheels on the ground and let's say a bucket at the top stuck to a pole. They put the rope around the bucket and pull the bucket all the way down to the base where the four wheels are with the rope. They tie it up and, at some point, somebody hits the rope with an ax and launches whatever's in the bucket toward the enemy. "Thrice towards thine enemy," I said we were talking about trebuchet.

The thing about a catapult is the very thing that holds it back, the very thing that sets it back is the very thing that releases it to maximum momentum toward the enemy. That's stress and tension. The rope pulls the bucket down to the base where the wheels add stress and tension to that bucket. That rope's full of stress and tension maxed out, tied up. The bucket's pulling on it, maximum velocity, and as soon as the trigger's pulled, the ax is hit, the rope is cut, it releases the bucket; the bucket launches the weapon, the weapon flies at maximum velocity, gaining momentum. Ultimately, when the boulder hits the ground, which was often used as the weapon in the trebuchet, it continues to roll…especially if they were shooting them downhill. It would gain momentum there as well.

You want to be like the boulder in that catapult. Maximum stress and tension pulls you back and at some point, or another, a trigger launches you forward and sends you to maximum momentum. Even when you run out of energy and hit the ground, you continue rolling forward until the catapult comes and picks you back up again. It maxes out your stress and tension. There's a trigger that releases you and pushes you forward. The catapult is a metaphor for life and the setbacks that come along with it. It's nothing more than a metaphor; that's all. Stress and tension builds up in your life. You go through a setback. Once you become aware of how the mentally tough look at setbacks—they break through it—maximum momentum happens.

Think of the quarterback. Stress and tension building up. The line is pushing on each other. They're growling; they're yelling; their pads are making a whole bunch of noise. The quarterback's taking 2, 3, 20 steps back, getting his arm cocked. The wide receiver's down there, throws the ball and makes the connection. There's your touchdown, but he had to go through maximum stress and tension. "Fuck, they're going to hit me! Block for me, motherfucker!"

Maximum stress and tension, the line's coming after him. The wide receiver still hasn't gotten far enough to outrun his coverage yet, and they're still not far enough down to where they can score on this final play. Maximum stress and tension, it's fourth down, and inches and they decide to go for a pass, and it's the end of the game. Maximum stress and tension on his arm pulling back. The shoulder muscles stress into their maximum tension on the backspin, launching forward, launching the ball, throwing the weapon, hitting the ground, continuing to run. Catapult, NFL, it's all the same, but I use CATAPULT also as an acronym, and I'll walk you through how to use it. This is an acronym for the mentally tough when you're going through a setback.

Commit to working through it. When you're in a setback, don't fucking become a victim. Commit to getting out of that shit. "Oh shit, I'm in a setback? I'm committed to getting the fuck out of here. I'm in a slump? Things ain't going my way? I'm committed to getting out of here."

You see, for the last month and a half, a lot of shit's been going down over here at Closerland. They lost the lease to my apartment. I got fucking jerked around on this fucking car deal. Lindsay's car, the company car that I fucking pay for as part of her salary, was hail damaged. It got beat to hell twice and then she had some flat tires, so we've had problems with that car. I was denied for three leases in a row in houses in Frisco, Texas, which is a city I was seriously considering moving to. I was trying to get a fucking lease there. I was denied for a bank loan for less money than I have in my fucking account.

How weird is that shit, trying to get some business built up? I don't need their fucking money, but I'm starting to get a credit score on my business. Regardless, I was denied for a loan, and I have a fucking business that will make probably $3 million this year. At least. We're just a day or two away from our first one for the year. They took my parking spots. We had to fire a bunch of people. We lost some fucking contractors. Then for the last month, it's been like a fucking beast over here in Closerland, but you don't hear me complaining like I'm some kind of fucking victim. I'll fight all them motherfuckers back because I'm mentally tough.

What I did was I said, "Hey, you know what? I see this shit storm's coming down on me right now. I'm going to get through this shit. I'm committed to get through this shit. I'm not going to let it faze me. I'm not going to let it hold me back. I'm going to let it set me back, but it's only building stress and tension because once I find the motherfucking trigger, I'm moving forward." C, commit to working through it.

A, admit responsibility. Earlier I talked about my emotions. I can't hide them; I'll turn my back on somebody quick as shit because of the three years that I spent in prison. Two years of it I spent in one of the worst fucking places you could ever imagine, man. When there were either 187 or 183 murderers in the year that I was there. It was fucking nuts in this place, right?

I learned not to trust anybody, so when I see somebody, I immediately think they're full of shit. I immediately think that they're a fucking liar. I immediately discredit other people's shit because I had been in a situation where every single day I was scared for my life, and I never believed a word anybody said because I knew that that's all they were going to do, try to take it from me if I wasn't careful. Get me caught up in some bullshit. Nobody was my friend there. The reason why I say that is so after you commit to working through it, you, A, admit responsibility. When I get myself in a setback, I want to ask these questions: *Why am I here? How did I get here?* Acknowledge where you are. *How did I get here?* Then: *How do I move forward?*

A lot of people never take responsibility; they never admit responsibility. "Fuck, I fucked up. I knew I should've done those calls. I knew I should've done this work. I knew we should've done this. I didn't commit here. I got lazy on this." I know that every time I've ever looked up in my life, and I weigh 185-190 pounds, this is because I hit the gym less. I should be walking around at 175 at all times, and I know anytime I'm at 10 or 15 pounds more on my frame, it's a lot because it doesn't go anywhere else other than my stomach. That's just the genetics. Ten to 15 pounds, a lot of people can lose that in 30 days. I can't. It's hard as hell for me, and I know that anytime I see that I have gotten up to that 185, 190 mark, which is a max for me, I'm always like, "Shit, I see what I'm doing. I'm cutting corners."

I have to admit responsibility. I can't say, "Well you know, I'm doing everything like I'm supposed to. I'm just being a victim here. It's just my genetics." No. You know what? It's time for me to step up. I fucked up. I got lazy. It took three months to get here. I got to get back and start hitting it five days a week. Admit responsibility. Your subconscious likes it when you know what got you in the situation and your subconscious likes it when you're confident enough to say, "Yeah, you know what? I fucked up. Let's move forward. Yeah, you know what? I fucked up. I'll own that. I'll take it." Because a lot of times, we spend our whole entire lives avoiding responsibility. "I didn't do it. It wasn't me. Oh, it's his fault."

Your subconscious actually likes it when you take responsibility yourself. You admit that it's your fault. You admit responsibility and move forward. Shit, your subconscious is like, "Yeah, you confident, cocky bastards, I love you."

Commit to working through it. Admit responsibility, then just tell yourself that it's temporary. You know, I see a lot of people get in these setbacks and these victim roles and these victim mentalities and these victim situations, and they say, "Oh, it's just how it is. It's just going to be this way. It seems like I'm never going to get through this." Life is long; setbacks are short; this shit is temporary. Tell yourself that. You have to program your mind.

As hokey as you may think this shit sounds, you have to program your mind to be able to get through setbacks because the key with the setback is like when the quarterback is taking those steps back, he's not walking back slowly. He's going through that setback as fast as possible. When the catapult's getting set up to launch the next boulder, they don't just slowly pull the damn thing down. No, they're loading the bitch back up, so they can fire it at the enemy again. The key is to get that setback down as fast as possible so that you can catch that momentum going forward, and programming your brain plays a huge part of that. So, tell yourself it's temporary. Then A, act as if you've already worked it out.

Put that shit in the past even if it's your current situation. Act as if you've already worked that shit out, and what I mean is, tell yourself it's temporary, and then work as if it didn't happen. Because often, if you'll tell yourself you're in a setback, you'll look for a reason to blame that setback for being in the situation you're in. "Ah, well, I would work a little harder but I'm already in the setback, so what fucking good does it do?" That's how mentally weak people think. Mentally tough people, you and I, we act as if we've already worked through it. We've worked through this shit, acted as if it doesn't matter. Act as if it never happened. Act as if you've already got this victory.

Speaking of that, P, put yourself in a position to win. Those two tie together really well, right? Act as if you're not going through that slump because you don't want to use that slump as an excuse. See, you've identified that you're there and now you're supposed to take action. A-C-T-I-O-N, action, you're going to act as if you're not in it, and when you're not in the slump, what do you do? You're working hard. You're in your zone. You're in your group. You're feeling it. You're making things happen. You're on fire. You're making it rain. You're dropping bombs. You're doing the big deals. That's the action you need to take. Act as if that's still going on right now. Act as if everybody wants to buy from you. Act as if everybody loves you and that you're on top of the world, and when you do that, that puts you in a position to win.

Let's think of it this way. A lot of people use the excuse, "Oh well, I'm in a slump, so I'm not going to do this." Instead, act as if the slump didn't happen, which will put you in a position to win. Keep moving forward. When you're in a slump, that's the best time to make the boldest moves. What do you have to lose? You're already under maximum stress and tension. You might as well compound that shit because it's going to feel the same. Put yourself in a position to win. Then you're going to utilize every ace that you have.

My friend Marshall Sylver says, "I play every ace I'm given." He's a hypnotist, magician, seminar guy from up in Las Vegas. He's a great guy, and because of the cards, his saying goes along with the stuff that he does. He says, "I play every ace that I'm given. I win by any means necessary. Anything that they throw at me that I can use for victory, I'll use it." Oftentimes, you'll get into a slump, or you'll find yourself in a setback, and you might say, "Well, I don't want to ask this person a favor." No; you should utilize everything. Put yourself in a position to win, to utilize every ace that you have. Get yourself out of there as fast as possible. Pull every favor you got.

I'm not talking about, "Could you help a brother out and give me a dime?" I'm talking about, "Hey man, listen. I need you to introduce me to such-and-such because I got a deal and I know that it's perfect for them." Utilize every ace you have. Pull every favor. Pull everything that you possibly can together especially after putting yourself in the position to win.

Then L, let the stress and tension build. The one thing that you see about the quarterback under all that stress and tension is that he's still mentally focused. He's still mentally tough. He's still got his eye on the wide receiver. He's still watching the line to make sure nobody breaks through and comes after him. He's still out there making sure that he's protecting his team. He's still watching the routes that the receivers will run. He's still in constant motion.

He's letting the stress build because he knows once it gets to the maximum amount, all he's got to do is release that ball, and it's a fucking touchdown. The catapult, stone cold boulder sitting in the bucket, it's under maximum stress and tension. As they're pulling that thing down there, letting the stress build, once that stress builds to the max, it's only a matter of time before the rocket's released, the boulder's shot. So, when that stress and tension are building in your life, just know that that's the beneficial point, right? You're going to use that for momentum. That stress and tension building up that you're going to re-channel into momentum. Let that shit build because you're going to knock the fuck out of it here shortly, which takes us to the last letter: T, trigger the momentum.

There's no sense in waiting for that trigger, right? If the boulder could fucking cut the rope itself, it would. The quarterback creates the trigger. He releases the football. He finds a spot, pivots maximum momentum; he creates the trigger by throwing the football. If you know what the trigger is, identifying the trigger is huge. "Hey, if I could just make XYZ happen, I could get out of this situation. Hey, if I could do XYZ, I could get out of this situation. If I make XYZ happen, if they buy XYZ, if I sell XYZ, then this is the effect of that. This is the direct result of that." Once you've identified that trigger, do your damnedest to make sure it gets pulled. Be that trigger. If you can't be that trigger, at least you put yourself in the position to win. Utilize every ace that you can until you can pull that trigger.

Let's go through this again. C, commit to working through it. Hey, listen, setbacks are temporary. You're going to get through it no matter what it is. I've been to some fucked-up places. I've done time in prison. I've been adopted and bankrupt. I've been homeless. I've been on drugs and didn't have any money, which is a shitty place to be in, right? When you have a drug addiction and no money, that's one of the most fucked-up places and positions you can be at in life, and I've been in a lot of fucked-up places and positions. I'm just telling you. Many people can resonate with that. That's a fucked-up position. When you've got a drug habit and no money, it's fucked up. But I got through all of it because it's temporary. Setbacks are temporary; life is permanent.

C, commit to working through it. A, admit responsibility. Just take responsibility. Your subconscious likes it. It feeds your ego. You, confident, cocky bastards. "Hey, it's my fault, my bad. I know what I did to fuck up. I won't do it again. I'm moving through this." Admit responsibility. T, tell yourself it's temporary. I'm committed to working through this. I know what I did to get here, and I'm going to work as if it never happened. A, act as is it never happened. P, put yourself in a position to win. I'm going to continue taking the motion. I'm going to push forward. I'm going to work harder than I ever have before, and then we're going to U, utilize every ace that you have. I'm going to call all my favors. I'm going to hit all my good clients up for referrals. I'm going to call this person, ask him for help, and I'm going to L, let the stress and tension build all the way to the max.

Stretch it out until there's no more so we can T, trigger the momentum. We can cause that release because we know once that trigger happens, it's over with. You pull the trigger. We're at maximum velocity and momentum moving forward. It's over with; you can't catch us. You get in our way; we'll fuck you up. That's exactly what happened. We're that boulder. If you get in our way, you will get fucked up because we are running full fucking steam ahead. We're out of this shit. We made the most. We made hay while the sun shone; we made the most of the bullshit. Life threw us lemons; we made lemonade. We have found a friend with vodka. We're fucking partying now, so CATAPULT.

Commit to working through it. Admit responsibility. Tell yourself it's temporary. Act as if you've already worked it out. Put yourself in a position to win. Utilize every ace that you have. Let the stress and tension build. Trigger the momentum.

Now that you've got a CATAPULT method, you've got to compartmentalize what just happened, so you can overcome the bullshit. You can refer back to that setback to help give yourself momentum for the future. Think of it like this, "Here's the lesson I learned from that setback," but you can't refer to it and let it damage you anymore. I can't let the fact that I was adopted, that my world fell apart…I can't let the fact that I went to prison, I can't let the fact that I went through divorce, I can't let any of those things fuck with me. I have to shut those off, file them in whatever file drawer there is inside my brain, and just like my two-thousand-and-fucking-nine tax returns; I'm not going to ever fucking look at them ever again.

They're there in case I need them, in case I fucking get

audited, but I'm never going to need them. There's no reason for me to refer to them on a daily basis, monthly basis or even ever again unless something regarding those 2009 taxes comes up. You have to compartmentalize this shit and get over it. Whatever it is that happened to you, it happened. It was a setback, and now you know what to do for future setbacks. If you go through a setback in the future or if you're in one currently, I'm sorry for you. But if you're in one currently, now you know how to CATAPULT your way out of the situation. Once you've done that, you're ready for the next phase: overcoming the bullshit.

There was a diagram. It showed how a woman's mind works and how a man's mind works. And a man's mind was all filed and organized properly, and the woman's mind was a drawer with a bunch of cables all fucking stuck together that weren't folded out. Ladies, because they're smarter than us are emotional beings. You're smarter than us, and your circuits all run together while we fold shit off, forget about it and move forward because we've had to. When we wanted out as cavemen, and the woolly mammoth chased us down and fucking scared the shit out of us, and we shit our pants, we still stabbed that motherfucker in the face and took him home to eat. If we didn't compartmentalize that thing, we'd be scared as fuck to go hunt woolly mammoths again.

Genetics, or Darwin, or the universe, or God, or whatever the fuck, blessed us men with the ability to compartmentalize our fears. Women, it's not so easy for you. In the cavemen days, women weren't the hunters for the most part. They were the skinners. They prepared the food. They took care of the family. They raised the children, while the men went out and hunted, gathered the food and stuff. You're taught to be more emotional. If an enemy came upon the cave, the natural reaction wasn't to fight back; it was to grab the kids, grab the goods and get the fuck out of there. Meanwhile, we men had to face our fears on a regular basis, and it was our job in the cavemen and Cro-Magnon days, to face those fears for our families. We had to compartmentalize that shit.

Ladies, what I'm saying is…this is going to be a little bit harder for you because you're not wired this way literally. It's not in your DNA. It's not in the genetics. And for many of you, it's not in the evolution of fucking womanhood. Guys, we get it naturally. Now, a lot of you motherfuckers choose not to fucking use it, but evolution gave it to us. It's going to be more difficult for ladies, right? I just want to acknowledge that, so you don't think that A) I'm being insensitive, or B) that I don't get where you're coming from. I do. I know what it feels like, and I can completely understand that I'm scratching the surface, but I just want you to acknowledge that I get it, because I can hear you right now saying, "Yeah, if it was only that easy."

The guys, I'm talking to you, we have the natural ability to do this shit. It was God-given to us. If you're not using it, then you're failing to utilize one of the greatest gifts that was given to us in our DNA. I taught Ash to ride with no training wheels today. It was kind of cool. Both my boys are riding bicycles now. When I'm teaching Ash today, he falls down a couple of times. He wants to quit, but as his dad, I tell him, "Hey man, you got to get your little ass back up on this bike and ride. I don't care if you're mad at me, I don't care if you're crying, I don't care if it skins your knees. I'm sorry you have to go through all that, but you got to get back on this, man. You got to overcome this fear. Come on. We're riding a bike today."

He's got me coaching him through it. The next thing you know, the little dude's riding all over the place. It's actually a really fun process, I have this little hoverboard and I ride behind him on the hoverboard, so I don't have to chase him and run. It makes it super fun, super easy, and then I can just roll up next to him and catch him. It's a pretty cool process. I do it with Jackson; it worked well, too. If you want to teach kids to ride without training wheels, I recommend buying a hoverboard. Be the best 500 bucks you're spending for a while anyway. But use that gift of compartmentalizing because you have to close that chapter. It's the only way you can.

"Hey, why am I here? What got me here? What can I do to move forward?" The only thing that you can do is close that chapter. You have to leave it behind you. If you're going to overcome something, then you're going to have to compartmentalize whatever it is that caused it and you're going to have to close the chapter on that bad boy.

I don't like doing shit twice. I'll do something once, and I'm good, and you can tell that by how I make posts in Facebook, by how I usually make comments and shit like that. I don't edit; I got people I pay for that at this point, thank God. So, my shit's so much better than it used to be.

I have good content, but I'm one and done. I hate doing shit twice. I hate turning around and doing something over. If I forget something at my house, to punish myself, I won't go back. And so, say I was supposed to grab some pants or whatever, I will go to the mall and make myself buy new pants and go out of the way and inconvenience myself so that I don't do that shit again. But guess what? I don't really forget much, but I hate leaving the house. If Amy left something, "I need to go back to the house, Ryan." "Fuck it, what do you want? We'll buy it somewhere else." I hate that shit. I hate going back. I hate doing stuff more than once because I've already closed that chapter.

When you're reading a book, you don't read the chapter and then go back after you finish the book and read that chapter again, right? That's not how any of us do it. It's not like, Og Mandino's *The Greatest Salesman in the World*, where you are supposed to read a chapter every day, then read the chapter before that. And that chapter that day and the chapter before that, like you've read the book basically every single day for a month. Most of us don't even do that shit, so we've done it once. We've extracted the lesson out of it; we're moving forward. You got to do the same thing when you're overcoming bullshit. We've done it once. We extract the lesson out of it; then we move forward. Then you have to get clear on what's the desired outcome.

You went through some bullshit. What does it look like when the bullshit's gone? You know what? Most people never thought about that, like: *this is what it looks like.* I was adopted, bankrupted, drugs, fucking prison, what does it look like when I'm not going through the bullshit? It looks like what you see in front of you. I own my own business. I have a beautiful wife. I have two kids, and I'm the fucking best dad in the world that I could possibly ever be. I try to be the best employer in the world to the people who work for me. Obviously, the best boyfriend and husband, whatever. Amy and I, we're in that period where if you're reading this, she might be my wife right now; we're engaged. I'm doing my best to show up everywhere. That's what it means.

The desired outcome for me was I'm free, I'm not on drugs. I have my own kids, raising my own family and running my own business. And guess what? Since I got clear that that's what I want, there ain't a damn one of those things that I don't have today. It's gold, right? It's just another gold setting, but if you don't know the desired outcome if you don't know what it looks like when you're not in the bullshit anymore, then how the fuck are you going to know? Then how are you going to escape the bullshit if you don't even know what it looks like when you escape? If I broke out of prison, how the hell would I know if I was free or not if I wasn't outside of the walls if I didn't understand what the fence was? How would I know that I have broken out of prison if I didn't know where the fence was, so I could realize that I was on the right side of it?

Some of you are going through the bullshit for longer than you should have because you don't know what it's like without the bullshit. When you get clear on what you want, you get clear on what you don't want, and your mind starts focusing on what you want more than what you don't want because that's how most of us are wired. And when you get clear on what you want, you start the attraction method. You start attracting. The universe starts to line up because you are clear. And your brain starts to look for it, and you have vision. But you've got to understand what that desired outcome is because if you're going to overcome the bullshit, you've got to understand what it looks like on the other side.

Here's the big reveal, though, and that's once you figure out the desired outcome, you've overcome the bullshit. You know where you want to be. You know what you want in your life. Whether it's short-term or long-term or what most people say: that you need a weekly goal, a 6-week goal, and a 6-month goal. But here's what I say. Goals are awesome, but you need to know what the desired outcome is. We self-sabotage. We're all guilty of it. Let's don't bullshit each other; we are all guilty of it because here's the thing. We'll go back to the beginning again. At seven years old, I learned that if you had a bunch of money, that it could be taken from you quick and your parents would give you up, and your whole life can fall apart in a minute. So, every time I got close to having money, look at what happened.

I started to get my shit together in 2005. When the feds kicked in my door, I caused the self-sabotage party. I know what the fuck I did because I have admitted responsibility. I was living out of my fucking league. I was in the wrong time. I should've been in Dallas. That shit would've never happened to me. I was trying to please people. I was self-sabotaging myself. I did not put myself in a position to win; I put myself in a position to fail because I didn't feel like I deserved to win. Have you done that? Have you subconsciously put yourself in a position to lose intentionally for fucking other people? For other people, that would probably continue to fuck you every chance they got?

There are really two types of people in this world: honest and dishonest people and honest people think everybody's honest and dishonest people think everybody's dishonest, and you wouldn't know one from another. So, if you're an honest person, you run into a dishonest person, you trust them. They think you're full of shit, so they fuck you over. If you're a dishonest person, and you run into an honest person, you think they're full of shit, so you fuck them over, and here they were trying to be one of the best people you could've aligned with in your life. We self-sabotage, man. I watched these guys at Warrior. Things will get great. They'll have the whole core four thing that Garrett talks about down in work and the next thing you know, they're over here, destroying their business. They're over here, cheating on their wives. They're over here, fucking up their car deal. They're over here, on a 10-day drug bender.

They don't think they deserve to win, so they want to put themselves in a position to lose because if anybody's going to throw a match, goddammit, it's going to be me. If anybody's going to throw the fight if anybody's going to fucking act like they got knocked out, stay down for a 10 count, it's going to be me, right? Better for me to fucking throw in the towel and sabotage myself than to let somebody else from the outside hurt me, right? How many of you have been in this position? How many of you thought this way before? How many of you have made it to a level that you wanted and then you didn't stay there, and it was your fucking fault, and you knew better, and you knew you were doing it and you sabotaged yourself?

That shit stops today, because once you become self-aware, once you know that that's in your nature, once you know that you mentally put yourself in a position to get fucked up, to lose, you know you put yourself in a position to where, if anybody's going to have control to throw in the towel, it's going to be you, you start avoiding that self-sabotage and become self-aware. "Oh shit, here I go trying to fuck another relationship." When Amy and I fight, that's the first thing I say to myself. "Here I go trying to run off somebody who cares about me because I don't think I deserve her. She's too goddamn good for me." And I'm not talking about how she's just pretty. Like, she's pretty, that's fucking awesome.

I don't know, Amy cooks dinner; she runs my freaking business; everybody loves her; she's super nice to me. I'm not a nice person for the most part. I fucking yell and cuss and get mad. You ask anybody, Lindsay, Roxanne, Amy; you ask anybody. I'm fucking hard to deal with. I get in my zone, and if you distract me, I get upset. I get mad. I'm fucking passionate. That's just how I fucking am, and Amy, she is a good-spirited individual who can deal with that shit like nobody I have ever met in my entire life. And when we fight, I'll try to run, because I don't think I deserve her.

Self-sabotage.

I have to tell myself, "There you go, Ryan. Trying to fuck up the one time you got in the right relationship with the right person. You try to fuck her up because you don't think she deserves this shit, but yet, you married three fucking people you should have never been with. Good job. Way to put yourself in a position to lose, you, dumbass."

I am self-aware, and I'm encouraging you to start looking at things that way, too, because when you admit responsibility and become self-aware... "Shit, it really is my fault. I really did do this. I put myself here. Here I am. I did this. Here's what I don't want. Here's what I want." ...It changes because that's what mentally-tough people do. Mentally weak people don't do that; mentally weak people sit there and go, "This keeps happening to me, and I keep going to prison, and I keep getting divorced, and I keep smoking pot. And I can't quit drugs and my parents, I ain't talked to them in five years...." Fuck all those excuses. I know why I got where I am. I know what happened along the way. I know what I do to destroy things and how I can avoid it because I'm self-aware.

Once you become self-aware, you can learn how to get over it fast. When you know that you got the bullshit and you know that you're in a position to win, and you know you're working through, and you're clear on what the outcome is, your job is to get to that outcome as fast as possible. Because as soon as you get the first win under your belt, the rest will follow. So, here's my encouragement. Whatever you're going through, go through it as fast as you can. Next time that you have to go through a setback, go through it as fast as you can. Speed the process up. The quarterback doesn't stroll those 2-20 steps; he doesn't casually take those 2-20 steps backward. He aggressively, quickly, rapidly takes those steps back and gets that play over as soon as possible; he gets that ball down the field as soon as possible; he gets that ball into the hands of the wide receiver as soon as possible.

As a matter of fact, the longer he's in the pocket, the more at risk he is. The longer he's hiding behind the line and has that ball in his hand; he's a fucking moving target. The sooner he can get that ball out of his hands and throw it forward to get it down the field, into the hands of the wide receiver, into the end zone, the sooner they can get back. The sooner they can continue moving forward and continue scoring and get another chance at scoring again the point after.

I took you pretty deep into this demon shit but remember there are three phases to overcoming and dealing with your demons. First, you have to identify where that demon came from. Childhood, past relationships, parents, authority figures, you name it. Use my CATAPULT method for getting over these setbacks, getting over these demons, getting through the bullshit, and then use what I just shared with you to overcome the bullshit. Do some self-discovery and figure out where those demons stem from, how you are going to get over them, and how you're going to break future setbacks that may be triggered. It's because of them.

Chapter #4: The New You

In this chapter, I'm going to discuss in greater detail how we can own our shit. We're not blaming anybody else. We have no excuses. The "no excuse" zone, that's exactly where we are at. There's no excuses. If it's meant to be, it's up to me.

You see, I've had every excuse to fail in my life, and I've given these reasons why I could have failed. You've learned from these exercises I've done myself, all these situations that I've been through. I have every reason in the world to fail, but for some reason, I haven't. Well, it's not for some reason. It's for a particular reason. I've refused to give up. I've learned my lesson each time I fail, and I've never really looked at things as if I've failed.

We were at the live Break Free Academy this week. We had about 38 people there. Part of my job at Break Free Academy is to find the technology that allows somebody to get up and running in the shortest amount of time possible, and it's not always the same for everybody, and I'm always looking for improvement. We use ClickFunnels, Leadpages, Pipedrive, leadPops. I switched all the loan officers and real estate agents over to something called leadPops. You can check it out at HardcoreCloser.com/leadpops. If you're a loan officer or a real estate agent, you may like it. I was teaching them what to do with it and how to use it strategically and why it was this way because I like it.

Some people were saying, (and this is how I am as well), "Wow. There's 32 funnels here. This stuff does VA, FHA, refinances, home search, home finders, home values. Dude, it does everything. It's awesome." And then there's—and I'm not hating on these people—but there's always one or two people in the room whose brain works like this: "But does it do this? Well, how come it doesn't do this?" It's always strange to me, because if you think about that for a second, it's like we're offering you 32 different ways for something to go right, and somehow your brain scoured through all those 32 ways that you could do something but found something you can't. Maybe you're like that. You have 15 blessings handed to you in a row, and you look for the one fucking thing that goes wrong with your life, and you become a victim.

If this is making sense right now, I'm probably talking to you, just like the preacher in church, "Oh, shit. He's talking to me." Or if you're me, I used to tell my exes, "Oh, shit. Pay attention. He's talking to you. Oh, shit. Did you hear that? You're making God angry. You better straighten up, girl."

Certain people tend to find that one thing wrong with a situation out of 32 different blessings—and again, I'm not knocking anybody from Break Free Academy Live—but what I'm saying is that's how your brain works everywhere. You've got all these good things going around you, and you focus on the one thing that's bad. Here's how I've been able to see the level of success that I have, here's how I've been able to get to the levels I am on financially, and spiritually (because I am a spiritual person). Those of you who know me, you know I have a weird belief system, but if I weren't spiritual, I would just be a complete anarchist nutjob, like I used to be. I'm not a religious person, but I am spiritual. I'm blessed financially. I have a blessed family. I've got a family of choice that I love today.

It's not my weekend to have Jax. Break Free Academy was Thursday and Friday, but I had Jax Tuesday and Wednesday, and then today I went and picked him up for two or three hours. We hung out with Roxanne and Tim and their kids over at Klyde Warren Park in Dallas. Jackson's mom had no problems and objected to nothing. "Yeah. Come get him." He called me, wanting to come over. That's still my family of choice. I chose to have Jax with Ashley. She's my family now, no matter if we're divorced or not because we have a kid together. Her family's my family. They're my family of choice. I took them in when I decided to have a kid with them.

I've been able to have all these things because when most people would say, "But I went to prison. That's a life-changing, a life-altering thing," I was like, "Man, this is a setback, but how can I make the most of this time? Shit, 15 months? Well, y'all send me some fucking books so I can try to get educated. I'm going to work out, create routines to take care of my body. I'm going to discipline myself since I have no choice but to eat right. That-a-way, when I get out, I'll eat right." Which, by the way, that shit doesn't work once you get out. There's too much temptation.

I never really looked at these things as failures because I've always looked for the blessings instead of the curse. Now, I'm not saying I'm an overly optimistic person. That's not what I'm saying at all. But I am a solution-oriented person, so I look for the solution. I'm sentenced to prison. The solution is to get educated and make the most of my time. That's the only solution. Everything else is out of my control. Hey, I've gone through a divorce. The solution is to be the best fucking divorced ex-husband, father figure, whatever you want to call it, in the world. Never have a child support payment late. Never not get my kid. Go above and beyond.

Jackson's mom doesn't pick up or drop Jax off. I do both. She doesn't bring him to our house. She doesn't come pick him up from our house. I do them both, and I have for three years now. I don't bitch about it. I just do it. If that's what it takes to keep the peace, a little thing doesn't matter because I'm looking for the one blessing. I could bitch about that, and I have every right to bitch about that. You might be saying, "Dude, this guy's getting raked by his ex-wife," but I look at the blessing in the situation, and the blessing is I get to spend time with my son. Fuck all the other shit. It's just some shit in my life I've managed.

Once you get successful, you pay the IRS. Fuck, they're the worst business partner in the world. You pay them a shit ton of money, like 20 percent, 30 percent of the fucking cash you earn, and when you earn a lot of cash, that's a lot of money. It costs a lot of money to earn a lot of cash, and then here's the IRS with their hand out. I want you to think about this for a second. It costs a lot of money just to be alive. You pay taxes just to be alive and functional and working. The fact that you have a job is a blessing, and then you pay taxes to be able to have that job. Look at kids then. Child support's just tax.

But the good news is, the taxes that I pay to IRS, I don't see shit for it. It goes to war, fucking cocaine smuggling, whatever the fuck those weirdos do, nerds that come look at a bunch of numbers on some papers, a bunch of fucking Harolds. I don't give a shit what she does with it, but I know that I get my son as a direct result of that.

I know that I get time with Jax. I pay child support, and I'm so scared of court. That's why I pay my taxes and my child support, too. I'm not here trying to be father of the year, paying taxes and child support, that shit you're supposed to do as your civic duty to live in this country, but what I'm saying is I look at the blessings behind those things in every area of my life.

I hate running. I hate working out. I hate that shit, but I love the results from it. I shouldn't say I hate working out. I enjoy it, but it's something that takes up a lot of time lately that I don't have, but I do it anyway because I love the results of it. I love the way it makes me feel after. During, I might want to puke my guts out. But after, I love the way that it makes me feel. I love the way that I get charged up as a direct result. I look forward to the blessing at the end of the workout more than I try to focus on the curse of getting the pain during the workout.

I just challenge you to shift your thinking, again. I've asked you to shift it four times in four different ways already, but I'm going to ask you to shift your thinking once more, to start looking for the blessings in things and stop looking for the one thing. If we give you 32 funnels, stop looking for the one thing that it doesn't do. If we give you 100 blessings, stop looking at the one fucking curse in your life and being a victim. You should be tired of it, and I fucking promise you everybody around you is tired of it. I don't say any of this to be an asshole, but I say this to be real with you.

I believe, in all reality, my calling is to teach people life lessons, but I like business better. I'm not going to lie. I do. It's not as deep. It's not as mentally exhausting for me. I've got some dark secrets just like anyone else. One of these days, I'm going to have to listen to that voice, and I'm going to have to heed it. This is me starting to submit to the voice. I'm a hardhead. But it doesn't matter. I am still starting to submit to that voice.

Now, you've got some foundation behind you from the prior chapters. Let's talk about the new you. I've covered not giving a fuck, covered being a high producer and dealing with your demons. Chances are, you're not demon-free today. We didn't just put you in the closet, and say what Richard Pryor did, something like, "Rub a cross across her pussy. Bitch get out of here," and the ghost was gone. We didn't do any of that stuff to you. We didn't exorcise the demon from you, but I gave you a specific pattern, a specific step for your life to where you can get rid of those demons. I didn't make you a high producer, wave a magic wand at you. I gave you specific steps that you could use to become a high producer.

What's going to happen is you're going to need to take in what I have taught you over and over again because you're going to forget 60 percent of it. I also taught you how not to give a fuck about anybody else, that once you stop caring about people, you start separating yourself from your family and your old friends and those people that you don't need anymore. And then you stop caring about what they say or what they think about you, and you start moving forward. Then when you've broken free of that bondage, you start producing a little bit more, and you already know the secrets to high production because I shared those with you. Once you start producing a little bit more, it allows you to have a little bit more freedom, believe it or not, because you're making more money to start dealing with your demons.

What happens when you deal with your demons? Man, if you slay the dragon, it's dead. When the hero gets the girl, the movie ends, but what happens there? Think about this. Let's just think about the movie *Tommy Boy*, greatest sales movie ever. In the end, Tommy Boy gets the girl. He saves the factory. They go on to get married, but then what? You see, six weeks prior to this, Tommy was a fat loser who couldn't get his shit together, and he'd spent seven years of his life burning through his dad's money in college. We see the end of the movie when the credits cut, and he ends up marrying the girl, and everything's awesome, or they're out on the boat. I don't know if they get married, but he gets the girl.

Now Tommy's this new person. His life changed. He went through a metamorphosis, but we don't see that. We don't see it in the movies. We don't see it in people in real life, and nobody talks about what to do at that point. They tell you how to be better, how to be better, how to be better, but what the fuck? What about once you become better? What if it's not about how-to anymore? What if you've got the how-to down and you've actually done it? Then what happens once you've become that new you? You've slayed the dragon. You're producing at the level you want to, and you've started only giving a fuck about the things that matter most, and then you become a new person. Instead of the credits shutting down, it's like, "Here's a bunch of how-to stuff now. Go how-to it. Here's the next phase and how to accept victory, how to accept success, how to move forward and continue to be that person."

See, it's one thing to have it. We all know the dudes that say, "Oh, yeah. Yeah. I had money one time, but then this business partner took it from me, and I ain't got no money no more," or, "I made a lot of money back in the mortgage days," or, "I made a lot of money back in the day." We all know somebody who had some shit. That's not what I mean. It's not that you were a high producer, or you didn't give a fuck. No. Listen, I want you to continue to implement and continue to grow and get better at what I'm sharing with you. I want you to be successful. That's why I put these resources together. Like DJ Khaled said, "They don't want you to win, but I do." I'm going to help you with what you have to do in the future in order to move on and own your shit and become the new you.

The first phase is you've got to become awake, and I don't mean awake in the sense of the alarm going off. I'm talking about paying attention to everything. When I drive, I ride a motorcycle, and it's scary. I've never been in a car accident. I may have gotten into a little bumper thing when I was 16, some bullshit. But I've never been in an accident that was my fault. I had a dude back into me when I was 16. I was in the car, but it wasn't my fault, so I don't know that it was an accident. Anyway, I've never hit anybody in a car with my car, and the reason why is because I'm awake. I'm aware. I'm paying attention. I'm hyper-aware of what's going on out there. I'm awake. You see a lot of people; they're not awake, and I'm not talking about this sheep mentality and all this other political shit that you might think I'm fixing to get into. I'm just talking about in general. They're sleeping.

Come on, man. We've all gone through the airport before, and we're like, "What the fuck is this clown doing?" It's ten o'clock on a fucking Thursday, and this piece of shit's wearing fucking SpongeBob pajamas, and he's fucking 40 years old. He looks like he ain't combed his hair in three fucking weeks. We see those people all over the airplane, the motherfuckers that when the airplane lands, they're in the corner seat next to the window, and they get up all hunched over and stand there for 10 minutes while they know the plane door ain't even open. And they're 30 rows back. We go to the store, and there are people just fucking casually looking at shit. Don't even realize that your cart is behind them, and you're trying to get around them. We go to the store to check out, and we realize the person there is just casually fucking scanning shit. They're not awake.

You see, here's the thing. I referenced waking up earlier in high production mode and getting shit done, and the fact that we have shit to get done and we have a higher calling and a mission is what caused us to wake up early. We're awake. Most people would rather sleep all day. Most people go out at night, get drunk, and they sleep an entire day. They go out, and the reason why they sleep an entire day is they're avoiding the hangover. They're avoiding the pain of being awake because being awake is painful. Life's not easy, nor is it short. We defamed that fucking myth. We demystified that myth a couple of chapters ago. Just like people sleep through hangovers, they sleep through life because life's painful. They do the minimum. We all know that one person who can sleep until noon.

I drank my ass off Friday night at the Break Free Academy graduation party. We drank six bottles, maybe ten bottles of liquor. I had my fair share. I tried my best to sleep as late as I could because, shit, I'm trying to sleep off the pain of a possible hangover, which I did not have because I hydrated. That's the secret. You're welcome for that. But I couldn't sleep past 6:30 a.m. You know why? Because I'm awake. I've got shit to do. I've got a calling. I woke up, grabbed a couple of people from my team, and went and did a recap, did a huddle. We met up and talked about what happened with the event and where we could improve for two hours. I'm awake. You need to be awake, too.

Now, let's talk about what it takes to be awake. First thing is you need to be intentional. At Break Free Academy, we talk about people on social media. Really, that's a metaphor for life, too, because what? How you do anything is how you do everything. That's right. Here's the thing. People get on Facebook, and they're just posting random pictures of their kids and dogs and news stories and pictures of themselves and all that shit. But those of us who are smart, and who are marketers, get on there and we post things intentionally; we post provocative things that cause engagement, calls to action which cause people to buy our shit—using indoctrination and cult-like vocabulary and building a following to where they are attracted to us, but we repel the people that we don't want around us, too.

We're intentional on there, and guess what? It's like being wolves. We're able to earn the sales on there. We're able to earn the respect online. We're able to deliver the stuff while everybody else is on there like, "Oh, hey. This is a cool picture. I think I'll share it." That's what a lot of people do for life, too. They just, "Oh, hey. This is cool," cruising through life. But those of us who are intentional have an extreme advantage because most people are unintentional. They do a bunch of dumb shit, and they're scared if they get caught doing a bunch of dumb shit they're going to have to own up to the fact that they're doing some dumb shit. So, they act like they're not intentional on anything. They conceal their intentions. That-a-way, when somebody catches them, they're just like, "Oh, they're fucking dumb."

I've seen it firsthand, many times in my life, with many people. Those of us who are intentional take risks, the risks of our intentions failing or whatever we had our intent behind not working out and looking like a fool and being judged, and that's not easy for most. But when you don't give a fuck like we talked about in chapter one, that's just part of it. Operating life from an intentional space changes the game, but you can't be intentional if you're not awake.

The next thing is, be authentic. A lot of people, again, conceal their intentions, and when you conceal your intentions, you're not being authentic. You're being something else because you're trying to hide. Being authentic is almost like being transparent. It's just; you are who you are. They see you. They get what they get. You have nothing to hide. I live in a glass house, metaphorically, with Facebook and my books and shit like that, but literally, too. The penthouse is glass. Being intentional and authentic, you don't have to hide anything. You don't have to remember a bunch of lies. Man, right now I know a bunch of people who have got a bunch of lies to remember. I know so many things about people, and I think this, *if I know this about them, how many other people know it, too? If I notice somebody's this way, how many other people do, too?* Because I'm awake. I'm intentional. I'm paying attention to everything.

When you're authentic, you don't have to remember what story you told last week because it's the same fucking story you're telling this week. When you're not authentic, and you're concealing your intentions, what happens? You're telling a different story because you forgot the one last week because most of us are shitty fucking rememberers. I told you, you're going to forget 60 percent of this, let alone the lies that you tell, and then those who mix the lies with alcohol and everything else make it even worse because you can't even remember the lies you told in the first place. And you don't even know a lie from a lie. Be authentic; be real with people. If people ask me a question, I tell them the truth.

Take this dude I was dealing with the other day. I said, "Hey, I'm looking for an apprentice. I want somebody to train to sell this shit. Somebody come to Dallas and literally do some *Fight Club* shit for five or 10 days." I had a few people offer. One of the guys shows up here at the house. I wasn't home. My doorman says that somebody's here, and I'm like, "Oh, shit." It's not what I meant to happen anyway. It's like 3 p.m. on a Tuesday. I talked to the dude through Facebook Messenger, and I asked him, "What are you doing? Are you selling anything?" And he gave me a bunch of typical, I'm-really-too-good-for-this-but-I-was-just-trying- to-be-cool-about-it types of responses.

I let the guy go, and today I just mentioned it, and somebody said, "Oh, man. If you didn't hire that guy, you're crazy." And I was like, "Well, first of all, we can think about the guy that didn't have anything to do at 3 p.m. on a Tuesday. He was here within five minutes. What the fuck? Second of all, we had some behind-the-scenes conversation. I think the guy was a loser." And I didn't mean he was a loser as in life. I don't know about that. I meant, a loser as in, he didn't make the fucking list. Well, he got all offended because he thought I meant loser as in life, and I just left it. I didn't even clear that part up, but for this. Here's the thing. I stick by the fact that he's a loser because he didn't make the list. He lost the competition that we were having. The reason why I tell you that story is I'm authentic. When I said it, I meant it, and I didn't have to lie to one person and say, "Oh, no. I thought he was a good guy." He might be. I don't know that well. Just through what I was asking for, he didn't make it, so he's a loser and didn't make the list, but I'm authentic about it. I don't have a bunch of stories to remember about a bunch of people. When the kid confronted me, I was just honest with him again. I've pissed a lot of people off with brutal honesty, but I don't have to remember lies, and people honestly appreciate it after a while.

I piss a lot of people off, but one of the funniest things and one of my favorite things, honestly, and not for reasons you might think, is when people hit me back up. They say, "Man, you pissed me off XYZ time ago, and I wanted to tell you to fuck off, and I hoped you died and your family was dead and everything else. But it never left my mind after you said it. Here we are six months later, and I'm just saying I'm sorry for all the evil things I prayed to happen to you." I get messages like that a lot, and I'm OK with that because I know I'm doing the right thing.

When people tell me shit, it makes me mad, too. Sometimes I'm like, "Man, fuck this guy. Fuck, he's right." I've apologized to a lot of people who were right, but I haven't apologized to a lot of people for standing my ground and being authentic. I'd rather be hated for being honest than loved for being a liar. That's tweetable, "Hated for being honest than loved for being a liar." Look, being awake is being yourself. When you feel your intention, you know you're authentic; it's just being yourself. Guess who the easiest person on this planet for you to be is? It's you. You're put here with this unique fingerprint and this unique way of doing business, and then we fall asleep. We sedate ourselves, and we do everything in our lives to become someone else.

I've tried to be the church guy. It didn't work out. I've tried to be the corporate banker. It didn't work out. I've tried to marry women who were the polar opposite of me, personality-wise. It didn't work out. I've tried to fit in all these different molds. It didn't work out. Once I started being me, and I'm like, "Well, fuck it. I'm just going to be this guy that I really want to be. I just want to be myself, man. I'm tired of putting a suit on if I don't want to put a suit on. If I want to put a suit on, great. If I don't want to, fuck it. I'm tired of hooking up with women who are the complete opposite of me, who don't get me. I'm done with it. I'm tired of hanging around friends who don't own businesses and don't have their shit together and don't want to do anything but party and go chase women. I'm done with that. That's not me."

I'm tired of being the guy who tries to go to church on Sunday and smiles and shakes everybody's hands when I'd rather be at home, drinking a beer, watching a football game, swimming or doing something else. When I started being myself, I got happy. Some people don't even know what happiness is. That's the crazy thing…you may think that you are content, but you don't know what happy is, like when you wake up every day just like, "Dude, I can't believe I live this life." When you wake up every day, and you're excited for the people in your life. I don't wake up every day and go, "Oh, God. The kids are going to get up." Dude, I wake up every day, and I'm like, "What's up, guys?"

I don't wake up every day and go, "God, I hope Amy doesn't wake up. She bitches all the time." No. I wake up in the morning, and I'm like, "I love you, babe. You're freaking awesome. Good morning," and guess what? Since I'm with a woman who's just like me, she's up, too. "What's up, babe?" She's not sleeping her life away either. She's on the freaking plan as well; she's on this ride, too.

I've got somebody who's just like me. I didn't attract Amy into my life when I was trying to go to church. I didn't attract Amy into my life when I was trying to be this corporate person, and that's what Amy was. She was a corporate person, worked for a hedge fund, but I attracted Amy into my life when I started being Ryan Stewman. Really, I attracted Amy into my life when I started being Ryan McCord, who I was before I was adopted. I felt like when I was adopted that I had to adopt this new identity, too, not just name-wise, but who I was, and I never found that person. But then I went back to the person I was born to be, the voice in the back of my head, the person I was told to be. Was it scary? Fuck yeah! It was scary.

I had to move into the extra bedroom of Ashley's parent's house, my ex-wife, Jackson's mom. I had to borrow money from them. It was embarrassing. We had to borrow money to pay our bills and shit because she didn't work. She was the polar opposite of me because I wasn't being myself. I was trying to be somebody else. Again, once I started being myself, I started telling it like it is. I started pissing people off. I made a few enemies over the years, but guess what? I was telling my friends when we're sitting at the park today that "You know what? Everybody worries about dying, and I don't, because most people have done a bunch of shit that they're scared they're not going to be let into heaven for, and I don't really feel like that."

Even if heaven exists—maybe it does. Maybe it doesn't. But even if heaven exists, and the guy that killed somebody on death row can repent for his sins five minutes before he goes in, but I've lived the life that I've lived my entire life, and I'm not allowed to go in behind a prayer, I'd probably rather hang out with people in hell anyway, because that's where my people are going to be. I'm not a religious person, so I don't really believe in heaven or hell, but either way, I've done what I'm supposed to do here, so I'm comfortable if I die.

I think we were talking about living forever. "Well, a lot of people want to live to be 100 years old." It's like, "Man, that's fucking old. I don't want all that. Gravity's a bitch." I'd rather go out on top. I'd rather go out maybe, not in my prime, but at the tip of the hill rather than all the way at the bottom. The reason why is because I've been myself this whole time. Not this whole time, but I've been myself the last 10 years. I've just been Ryan. I've for sure been Ryan since 2010 when I didn't have a governing body over me anymore, no more parole, no more corporation. I can tell you, it's been easier and more successful being Ryan than it was trying to be somebody else when I was trying to fit into all these different boxes that I thought society wanted me in, but that was something that I had to be awakened to. That was something that I had to wake up and realize. Again, being awake is part of it, paying attention, being intentional, being authentic, being yourself.

The last sense of being awake is looking for advancement. If you're going around intentional at work, in life, and with your family, one of your intentions needs to be for constant advancement. You see, some people will say you're greedy, and I didn't say constantly ripping somebody off or constantly hurting somebody. I said constant advancement. How can you get better? How can you advance? How can you get to the next level? How can you go forward? How can you grow? How can you advance? See? That needs to be one of your main intentions. You need to look for every opportunity for advancement. When things come my way, I don't look for how it can hurt me. I look for how I can use it to advance. Software comes along; it makes my life easier. Can it advance Break Free Academy and make it that much better?

Oh, we've got membership sites, networks, and capital partners. Oh, we can advance The Tribe. Oh, we've got ClickFunnels now, and it's better than Kajabi. Oh, we can advance our digital program division. Everything I do, I look for advancement. I don't look at it as, "Oh, Kajabi, they changed their platform. It's the end of the world." No, instead, it's *what's a solution to this? How can we use this for our advancement?* So, we moved to ClickFunnels. Most people would be bitching that Kajabi did some dumb shit and changed their software, and we complained about it. We have every right to complain about it, but at the same time, we looked for the position to advance.

We joined up with Russell Brunson and got involved with ClickFunnels. We have advanced because we were intentional about what we were doing. What can we do to make sure we advance? That's our intention in everything. Our motto over at Hardcore Closer is, "Total optimal profit." We're always looking for advancement. In anything that hurts you, there's a chance for advancement. In anything that frustrates you, there's a chance for advancement. In anything that gets in your way, in any roadblock, there's a chance for advancement.

Two weeks ago, everything was falling apart on us. Taxes didn't get filed. They lost the lease. They stole our parking spots. Everything was coming down. We lost a couple of people on the sales team. It was the end of the world, but I said, "This is a chance to grow. What are the lessons learned here so I can advance?" I look at it with intention. *All right. All this shit's happening.* My intention is constant advancement. *Where can I grow? All right. Here I am. This is what's going on. This is the reality of what I'm facing. This is the shit that's happening right now. What can I learn from it, and how can I use it for advancement?* If you'll play that role instead of the "Oh, no. I'm a victim. Oh, why is this happening to me?" you'll find more success. Try saying instead, "How can I advance from this?"

This is a lot better position to be in in life than "Why is this happening to me?"

It's like I noted in a prior chapter, "You're going to listen to this shit, and you're going to make a decision whether you believe what I say or not." Well, that's bullshit. What if I'm right? I mean, worst-case scenario, I'm not. Shit's the same, but what if I'm right? You'll change your fucking outlook from a victim mentality to look for constant advancement. It changes the game.

Let's assume you're awake now. You're intentional. The next step is to be aware. When I was in federal prison, they woke us up at 6:00 every morning with this bell, and at 6:15 the door opened, and there was another bell, like a school bell. When you woke up, you had to be wide awake because when you walked down the hall, you could get in a fight. You could get jammed up by a prison guard. You could see people having sex in their cell. You learn not only to be awake, but you learn that next phase, to be aware. Aware of what's behind you, not worrying about it, but just aware. Aware of what's in front of you, not concerned about it, but aware. Aware of what's going on all around you with 360-degree vision. You have to be aware of areas of your life.

The first thing you need to be aware of is your alignment and intentions. I know some high-level people in my life these days. I have conversations; oftentimes, people ask me business-related questions that I had learned from them in the past. Some of my friends that are constantly in trouble with business partners and swapping ventures and everything else are an example. They'll make good money and start something up, and then destroy it because a partner ripped them off, and it's always the partner ripping them off. It's always, "This person stole from me," or, "This person did that."

I tell them all the time, "Hey, man. You are who you attract. If you're trying to be this way, you attract people who are that way into your life. If you're trying to be somebody you're not, you're not authentic." Going back to the awake part, if you're not authentic, and you're not being who you're supposed to be, you're not being the real you. You're attracting other people who are not who they're supposed to be. You're not being the real you, so your relationship is born, from the beginning, on some fucking fake bullshit, and both of you are fake to each other and don't even know each other. What happens is, over time, when you start to get comfortable, you start to know each other, and then you start to resent each other because you realize you're both pieces of shit.

I hate to say it, but that's what's going on. That's what most alignments are like. "I'm fake. You're fake. OK. Let's both agree to be fake, even though we know we're both fake, and let's keep that agreement, and we'll be fake in front of other people, so they know we're fake together. And you keep my fake-ass secret with your fake-ass promise to keep it. Fake agreement? Shake fake hands." Then you wonder why your business partners rip you off. They're fake. When they said, they weren't going to rip you off. You're fake, too, though. You pretended like you were a big man, money man. They pretended like they knew what to do with that shit, and then they didn't, and you get mad that they split your money, when both of you were lying from the beginning.

I've seen that happen 100 times. I've seen it happen more than 100 times. Your alignments take precedence over your assignments. Whatever you're supposed to do here on this planet doesn't matter as much as who you do it with. Think about that. Your alignment takes precedence over your assignment. Who you do things with on this planet is more important than what you do.

The next thing that you need to be aware of is your habits. I was at an event a few months ago and saw one of the greatest sales pitches I have ever seen. In the beginning, the speaker said, "Here are personal deal-breakers." I don't remember what he called them, but he said, "They're personal deal-breakers. Be aware. Pay attention because when I say things about money or when I say things about business or I say things about buying things or investing, look for yourself to start getting fidgety. Look for yourself to get up and go to the bathroom. Look for yourself to start getting on the phone. Look for you to tell yourself that it's not for you. Look for an excuse not to take action. Look for your habits and how you get uncomfortable in these situations. What other areas of your life is that showing up in?"

I thought, *well, hot damn. Hey, that's a hell of a way to give a seminar.* It's true. Are you aware of your habits? Let's talk about the partner thing again. A lot of people build businesses up and then find a reason to destroy it; they need a problem to solve. Are you aware that your habit might be that you like solving problems more than you like running businesses? If that's the case, maybe you should be a consultant and fix other people's problems instead of building businesses up and then fucking them up, so you have more problems, and then not having the capital to solve the problems. Why don't you go fix other people's problems, and then when you're done fixing their problems, you can move onto the next one? That would be a more logical thing for you to do, as opposed to what your habits consistently get you to do, which is to go fuck up your own business because you get it running smoothly, and you don't have any more problems. Then it drives you crazy because you like solving problems. Sound familiar?

Your habits—how you work out, how you do things in the morning, what you do with your time, how you manage your time, how you manage your business, how you manage your life, how you manage your family—look at your habits. I'm not just talking smoking and healthy eating and all that shit. I'm talking about your habits overall; I'm talking about your routines because here's the thing. You've got to be aware of them because how you do anything is how you do everything. I keep repeating it because it's true. You show up in one spot; it shows up in another, and I look for it. Smart people who are awake and aware like myself look for it. I look for how somebody does one thing to how they do another. I had to have a confrontation with a guy the other day. This was a stupid situation, and I had to have a hard conversation with him. I knew it was going to be confrontational because he wasn't going to hear what I had to say to him.

I'm authentic and comfortable with myself, so I don't mind having those tough conversations. I'm surely not scared of them like most people are. Whatever you could say doesn't really hurt my feelings because I know it ain't me. If it is and it does hurt my feelings, I'll fix it. I'll become better at it. I'll grow. I'll look for advancement. I have a lot of hard conversations, and I noticed this person was covering up the real conversation. I told the person, "I bet you do that a lot. Somebody starts getting serious with you, and you start dragging it somewhere else, back up on the surface. I bet that shows up a lot in your life because how you do anything is how you do everything, and I bet if you just stayed focused on one thing instead of trying to drag somebody's attention off on something else, you'd get more stuff completed."

I went through this whole conversation with him, and I noticed, man, if you cover up over here, what else are you covering up? If you're a hard worker over here, you'll be a hard worker over there. If you're a liar over here, you'll be a liar over there. If you're a short-cutter or a lazy person over here, you'll be a short-cutter or a lazy person over there, because how you do anything is how you do everything.

The last part of being aware is being aware of the lessons. It's part of advancement. Let's say failure happens, what's the lesson? I know when I went to prison the second time, it was a huge failure for me. I didn't even know I was in trouble. I'm like, "What the fuck? I was told you could have a gun," and they're like, "Well, Texas says you can. The ADF says you can't." It's kind of like weed in Colorado. Colorado police won't do anything about it, but the DEA can still bust you, and you're just in one of those snafus, man, like, "It sucks to be you." Yeah, but why did Texas kick my door in?

It opened my eyes to: "Hey, the lesson is if I'm going to do anything that I'm unsure about, or that there can be a gray area on when it comes to law, I'm just not going to do it." The lesson for me was, "OK. I was removed from the mortgage business and put in a situation, so I didn't lose my mind." The lesson for me was I was aligned with the wrong person and the wrong wife, and I had to be removed from that situation, and that was the only way that that was going to happen. Where are the lessons here? Where can I advance my life? Lessons are often painful, so we avoid learning them. Lessons are often hurtful and strenuous, like most anything else in life, so we try to sleep them off and ignore them.

If you're awake, you're not sleeping, and you're aware of the lessons that are learned within your failures, your shortcomings, your setbacks, your issues and your problems. If you start looking for those lessons and how you can turn those lessons into some form of advancement, A) you have to be awake to look for that in the first place, but B) it changes the game for you. Don't look at things as a curse or a blessing. Look at them as a way that you can learn a lesson. There's another tweetable thing for you, "Don't look at issues as a curse or a blessing. Look at them as a learning lesson." When you start looking for lessons, lessons teach us. We learn; we become more educated. We get experienced. We're one step closer to becoming an expert. Extract the lesson, remove the emotion, and advance.

Now, the third part. OK. Here's the part where we move on. You've got all this how-to stuff. What happens after the curtain closes? Here it is. You've got to learn to be awesome. You're already awesome, so I'm not talking about picking up another personality and trying to be something else. You've got to learn how to deal with it. I shit you not. When you realize that you love yourself, and you're awesome, and you're OK, and you're awake, and you're aware, and you're comfortable in your own skin, and you don't give a fuck what people say about you, and you're in your own lane doing your own shit, you become an awesome motherfucker. Maybe to people around you, or maybe not, but it doesn't matter. You become an awesome person anyway. Your subconscious and your conscience fall in love with each other. You love yourself, and you're like, "Man. Nobody else knows the work that we've put in here, but I've got your back. Nobody else knows what we do behind the scenes but me and you, conscience and subconscious. I've got you."

What happens is a lot of people get to this point, and they don't know how to deal with being awesome. They don't, so they destroy themselves. They stop working out. They get fat, or they get thinner. They develop drug habits. They develop drinking habits. Things change for them. They can't deal with it. But I'm going to share with you, how I'm OK with saying that I think I'm awesome, and so is everybody else who hangs out with me. I'm sure there are people out there who don't think I'm awesome. I probably don't like them either, but to me, I'm exactly who I want to be. I'm exactly where I want to be in my life, right this minute.

Do I want more? Absolutely, but right now, I'm exactly where I'm supposed to be and exactly where I want to be. Do I want to be somewhere else in the future? Absolutely, but right now, if you were to go back a year ago and you were to ask Amy, or you were to record my life a year ago, you could probably look on YouTube and see that I said it, I am exactly where I fucking wanted to be. And now I have bigger goals. A year from now, I'll be exactly where I want to be then, too, because I'm OK with being awesome.

First and foremost, I love myself, and I'm not talking about in some "look in the mirror and jerk off" kind of fucking way. No. I'm just talking about I'm OK with who I am, and I'm happy with myself. Despite all the bullshit that's happened to me in the past, or any bullshit that'll come against me in the future, I'm OK with me, and I love myself. I'm extremely happy with who I am, and it didn't happen that way overnight. I spent most of my life destroying shit because I hated myself, because I was being someone else, and I hated that person that I was being. But I felt like I had to be that person in order to maintain the relationships and the balance and everything else. It just drove me to a point where I fucking cracked, and I said, "You know what? I want to be this person."

Then when I started to be that person more and more (and I am that person today), I started to like that person. I stopped hating myself. I started loving myself, and the universe started lining up for me, and it's not some hokey shit. I'm telling you what if I'm right? What if it's that simple and that is the answer? What if it unlocked that shit? The worst thing that can happen is I'm wrong, and it doesn't work, and you stay where you're at right now. But what if I'm right and you try it, and it works for you? What if you become who you're supposed to be, not who society wants you to be? Not who your parents or your boss or anybody else wants you to be, but you become who you're supposed to be, and you love that person, and shit lines up for you? What if that's how it works? Not become who you want to be, not become who they want you to be, but you become who you're supposed to be? You fall in love with yourself and advancement happens.

You see, that's what happened for me. But you have to prove to your subconscious that you love yourself, because often we say, "I love myself," but then we do shit that clearly reveals that we don't love ourselves, like putting others first. Man, this goes against what a lot of people say. They say, "You know, you've got to put others first," and while I'll agree that it's nice to put other people first, that can't be your full-time mission. Your full-time mission has to be for constant advancement. That means that you have to be first. The leader is first. The first one through the line takes one for the team. You have to do you first. You have to show yourself that you care about you first. If you don't want to do something, don't do it. If you want to do something, do it. If somebody's asking you for something and you don't feel comfortable, don't do it. Tell them. Be comfortable in your own skin. Be who you're supposed to be.

When you do shit that you don't want to do for other people and to keep balance and to perpetuate lies and shit like that, you're showing yourself that you don't matter, because you're putting other people's feelings above your own, and you can't do that. I know that probably goes against everything you hear in church and school and everything else, but it doesn't work that way. If church and school work so fucking well, how come we have the problems that we have? If church and school work that well, how come every country doesn't have them? You say, "Well, they're developing countries." Whatever. Church and school are half bullshit. We know that. Even those of us who go to church on Sunday know that half of it's bullshit. Even those of us who have degrees know that half of it was bullshit.

When you start putting you first, guess what? Other people start putting you first, too, because they are in the same situation. They're trying to be people pleasers and pretending to be somebody else. Again, I don't say any of this from a narcissistic standpoint. I'm just telling you. Do you think Steve Jobs woke up in the morning and he was like, "Hey, all the people that use iPhones, man, we're going to put them first"? No. Steve Jobs woke up in the morning, and he said, "This is what I've got to do to be able to free me up so that I can do my thing so that these people can have these phones." He put himself first, died at the top of his game.

The other thing about being awesome is you get to focus on winning. You know what's awesome? Winning. It is. If you don't think winning's awesome, then I don't know what to tell you. You have to focus on winning. Focus on personal wins. When you put yourself first, you win. "I've got that. Well, that worked out in my favor." Winning, that's a win. When you start focusing on personal wins, you put yourself first. We tend to get to the top, get the girl, become the hero, then we find some way to damage it all, beat her up, get a divorce, got two kids, living in a trailer park in a van down by the river, because, for all we know, that's what happened with Tommy Boy. We didn't see the curtains close on that. But to avoid that, put your focus on the wins.

Most people, in life, are asleep. They're unintentional, and they're focused on their losses. They can't figure out why they keep attracting more losers. They can't figure out why they keep attracting more losses because that's what they get focused on. See, you keep what you're focused on. You have what you focus on. I focused on being right where I am today a year ago. I stayed focused until I got here. Now, I'm focusing on something bigger. I'll stay focused on that until I get there. Focus on the wins because if you start focusing on the losses, you'll focus on the bad shit. You're not going to be able to keep up your awesomeness. Negative people are not awesome. People who focus on being a victim, people who focus on losses, people who focus on the things that don't matter, they're not awesome. You know what's awesome?

Winners. Everybody fucking loves a winner. You know what's even more awesome than that? Winning.

What I'm telling you right now is you've got to love yourself. And you'll prove that to yourself by putting yourself first. Focus on every single win that you get, not your losses.

Lastly, concentrate on swinging singles. Garrett J. White says this often. He says, "You swing singles. You focus on the small wins. You get a base hit, and you get another base hit. You get on base every time. You're going to eventually score." Many of us are trying to focus on home runs or trying to get the big win. "Oh, the big win is $10 million in my bank account," and you ain't got $10 in your bank account. Let's hit a single. Let's get 100 in there. Let's get 1,000 in there. Let's start hitting singles. Let's get another 1,000 in there. Let's get another 1,000. We'll get this shit to add up to a million eventually, but if you keep swinging for that million, it's not going to exist.

So many people are out there trying to step up and hit a home run, and they end up striking out. Even the best guys in Major League Baseball strike out more than they hit. I don't know. That may not be true. I don't know enough about baseball to say that. It feels like it, though. You watch it; it always looks like it's 3-to-5 up and 3-to-5 down. Somebody's striking the fuck out all the time. Do they focus on the strikeouts? No. They focus on the wins, but more importantly, they focus on swinging singles. You know why? Because that's what puts people on base, that's what scores home runs, that's what puts runs on the board. Many of you struggle because you've got this big-ass audacious goal, and that's what you've been taught forever, "10x your goal." All right, that's fine, 10x it, but let's swing singles to get to the damn thing.

One of the things I had people do at Break Free Academy was write down their sales processes, in other words, what happens from start to finish. In a room full of people, nobody had ever written it down before. None of them. It happens every time. I tell them, "Now you've got single movements instead of just selling something. Now you've got a single process, single steps across the whole way. That's how you win. Games are won by swinging singles."

Let me recap the parts to dealing with the new you. You've got to be awake, intentional, authentic as yourself and look for constant advancement. You've got to be aware. Be aware of your alignments and aware of your habits because how you do anything is how you do everything. More importantly, you've got to be aware of the lessons attached. Learn the lesson. Gain the experience. Take the advancement. You have to realize that you're awesome. To do that, you've got to love yourself. You've got to put you first, and that's really how you show yourself you love yourself. Focus on your wins. Focus on your personal victories. Look at the 10 things that went your way, not the one thing that didn't go your way. Look at the 10 things that worked, not the one thing that's missing. Look, if you're going to hit a big-ass goal, the way to hit it and the way to get there is by swinging singles.

You've got the tools and systems to be this new person. Be who you're supposed to be. Show up in life as who you're supposed to be. Don't show up in life as who you want to be; don't show up in life as who they tell you to be but show up in life as who you're supposed to be. You'll find yourself falling in love with yourself, and you'll find yourself advancing. It's amazing how it all lines up.

You may think I'm crazy. You might think, *oh, he's all full of shit.* Well, what if I'm right? I know I've repeated that many times, and it's for a reason, because I know if I repeat something enough, it'll stick in your head, and it won't be some of the 60 percent that you forgot. I want you to think when you're trying to figure out whether you're actually going to do this shit or not...what if I'm right?

Chapter #5: Upper Limits

This chapter concerns upper limits. If you don't know what that is, an upper limit is something that I wasn't sure what it was my entire life, either. I'm going to teach you where the root of it comes from, how to identify it and then how to move on and press through them. I wasn't sure what to call these. I have had upper limits for my entire life on everything. I'll retell you some stories that will reiterate some of these anchors that I've set in my brain.

I was with Garrett J. White, and we were having a couple of drinks over at this place called Mozambique, which is in Laguna Beach.

We were sitting on the top of the Mozambique's roof, and he mentioned the word "upper limits." He said, "It's almost as if it's some kind of upper limit." I had never heard that before, and I thought that was a really cool idea and a cool way to phrase the conversation that I'm going to speak to. An upper limit is when you peak, and then you tell yourself you don't deserve that peak. It's when you get to a level and then you peak and put a limit on yourself. There are two ways that they can race NASCAR. There's with restrictor plates and without. One way puts a limit on how fast things go; the other way puts no limits on how fast they can go.

My goal is to help you identify these areas of your life where you hit upper limits, so you are able to push through them. Because I have had many upper limits in my life that I've had to learn to push through. Like everything, action solves most of your problems. There are two things that solve problems: action and money. Usually, money comes from action. Go ahead and tweet that. Two things that solve your problem. Usually, money and action. Money comes from action. The thing is we are all programmed with these upper limits, and the goal is to pass through them. But what is the root of an upper limit?

You see, an upper limit is when we get to a spot where we feel undeserving of what's going on in our lives, and we've got to find some way to get rid of it. Let me give you an example. Have you ever saved up a significant amount of money? It felt uncomfortable. Have you ever gotten a big-ass paycheck, and then bought a bunch of dumb shit that you normally would have never bought? You knew that you needed to save money, but for whatever reason, psychologically, you didn't feel comfortable with having a certain dollar amount in your bank account. I'll give you a personal example.

In 2008, I was released from federal prison. I had zero dollars in my bank account. Throughout the first three or four months of me being released, I had zero dollars in my bank account. Every dollar I got went right out the window, trying to do everything that I could to get ahead, right? I got used to, through prison and through this 90-day, 120-day struggle period that I went through, not having money in my bank account. I got the pattern down; every time I got money, I paid it right back out somewhere because I owed it around town.

That became subconsciously ingrained in me. When I started actually making money, I would get $3,000 or $4,000 in my savings account. I'd find something stupid to blow it on: vacations, jeans, clothes, jewelry, more vacations, this club, whatever, else. Helping friends out, stupid investments. The whole thing was I had trained myself to get rid of every dollar I had because that's what I had been doing all this time.

You might be going through a phase where every dollar you have goes out the window. There's going to be a time when that's not the case anymore. You've got to make sure that you're identifying that upper limit in the future. I had upper limits ingrain that in me. At a younger age, as I've mentioned, my grandparents, both of them became millionaires. Then, within a few short years, the savings and loans crashed. Their loans came due. We lost all of our money. An upper limit anchored in my mind at that time even at a young age.

I challenge you to think back and identify these areas, why we do the things that we do. You think about upper limits: money in our bank account. *Oh, man, my check was too big. I got to spend some of it. Oh, man. I'm not comfortable with $10,000 in my bank account. I got to spend some of it. Oh, man. I'm not comfortable with having this chick. I've got to cheat on her. Oh, I'm not comfortable with having this girlfriend. I've got to be mean to her. Oh, I'm not comfortable with having a husband that's making this much money. I have got to cheat on him. Oh, I'm not comfortable with having this significant other that's making this much money. I've got to be mean to him and be a bitch to him.* We all have these upper limits that we hit.

I'll be real with you. With my past spouses, I was in relationships where I felt like they were lucky to have me; it was a superiority thing. Now, I'm in a relationship where I feel lucky as hell to have Amy, and I hit upper limits there pretty constantly because I feel like I don't deserve it. I remember when I first had $20,000 back in 2009. I had finally saved up some money, gone through the whole 2008, getting out of prison thing. In 2009. I had $25,000 in my bank account. The only reason I had that money there was because Jackson's mom hit me up every day and made sure it was there. Jackson's mom made sure I couldn't

221

spend that money because she knew I would. I'm this way still. Amy watches out for me now. If I get my hands on stuff, I'll start to spend it.

In the past, I'd saved up $200,000 in cash. The local police department kicked in my front door. My ex-wife took it all while I was in prison. I had started establishing these anchors, especially with money. Adam Stark and I were talking the other day. He said, "Man, you know, it was really hard for me to save up money to hit six figures in my bank account. I'd get up to 85 or 90 thousand, and I'd find some dumb shit to spend it on." He goes, "I finally just had to accept that I needed to save my money and that it needed to be there. I needed to get comfortable with it in my bank account." It's the truth. A lot of you would have more money, without the need to go to Amazon and buy shit. It's not the need to invest in stupid shit that you know that's not going to work for your business. It's not buying the piddly shit that you use once and throw away or upgrade on the latest phone.

It's not that. It's all upper limits. It's ways for you to spend money on stupid shit so that you can get back down to a comfort level that you're OK with. I touched a little bit on the roots, but ask yourself where did you peak? Where are those anchors coming from for you? Where have you peaked in the past that you don't feel comfortable going past now? We're less than

$15,000 away from breaking a million dollars this year in the beginning of July here at Hardcore Closer. I struggled before because my best year previous to this was $700,000. It wasn't last year. It was years ago, in 2005; $773,000, and once I got there, I felt like I'd peaked. I'll be damned if I couldn't get past it again. I had to come to grips with my upper limits.

My upper limits this time consisted of how much money could I spend to build a team? Once I started breaking through these upper limits, this million-dollar per year, million-dollar per half year empire that I'm building, it's starting to actually come into play. Here's what usually happens. The root of these upper limits, these things that have happened, in my case, my grandparents losing money, me going to prison when I was at the top of my game, all of these things that have happened established these upper limits. Guess what? We like to set them on ourselves and other areas that don't even apply. Have you built up a business that was making you some money? You had everything in the world going for you, and you fucked it up for no reason. You got mad, fired this person. You look back, and you're like, "Dude, what the fuck was I even mad at that guy for?"

I had a business partner. Man, the world was going for him. He had everything at his feet. He was making more money than he'd ever made before. Everything was perfect. He wasn't comfortable on that level, and he had his upper limits. What happened was drugs settled in. He started to blow his money because he couldn't have it around. You run out of things to spend money on when you're making money, and you have upper limits. You don't want to save money. Look at the *Wolf of Wall Street*, Jordan Belfort. He had some serious upper limits, but he was making so much money. He didn't know what to do with it, too. He had a beautiful wife. It was drugs and hookers, right? Upper limits. He'll tell you this. You can ask him.

I'm not talking shit about the guy, but that's a prime example. So much money that he was trying to get rid of it, trying to get it overseas. He knew that everything he was doing was illegal, and if he would have just paid taxes on it, he wouldn't have had to deal with any of that shit. Instead, upper limits settled in and made him do a bunch of dumb shit because here's what we do, right? These upper limits set in. Once we hit the upper limit, we decide to destroy the foundation that we got there on. I'll ask you again, have you built businesses and destroyed them? Have you intentionally sabotaged relationships and networks that would have been awesome for you? You did it, and you're like, "What the fuck did I even do that for?" But you did it. You've done it over and over again.

We hit these upper limits, and we destroy shit: relationships, businesses. A lot of it has to do with the words that we use. Not everything stems from the words we use, but a lot of it has to do with them because there are these phrases we've heard our entire lives, "Money is the root of all evil," so when we start to get a whole lot of it, we start to associate that with evil. When we say things like, "Money can't buy you happiness," in our mind, it's like, *hey if I have all this money, I'm not going to be happy.*

Those things have been plugged into many of us at a young age. Then, we've seen tragedies happen. People win lotteries. People get insurance settlements. People get all these great deals of money, and then fuck them off. How many times have we seen, again, people win the lottery or people become big-time rock stars or people become big-time celebrities and make lump sums of money, only to turn around and get addicted to drugs? Only to turn around and blow it on gambling, or on weird hookers and blow? The normal things.

We see a lot of people like Tara Reid, for example. Once, she was one of the hottest chicks. Everybody wanted to choose the *American Pie* chick. Everybody wanted to be with Tara Reid. She hit that upper limit, man. Drugs, blew all her money, doing a bunch of crazy stuff. She'll never get it back. It's what we do. We build and destroy because of these phrases of life.

Money is the root of all evil; money can't buy you happiness. A rich fool can't go through the eye of a needle as easy as a camel, or whatever, right? There's all these things that we say. The truth is those are the upper limits of others being passed down upon us. That's generational upper limits.

Now that we know what the roots are let's define the reasons upper limits exist. The number one reason is low self-esteem. We don't think we deserve that temple, right? We hit these upper limits because we don't feel like it's where we should be. We don't feel that we've earned it, especially in the sales world. Somebody has a bad-ass month. They close a bunch of deals, and they're like, "Oh, dude. The manager gamed them. He spoon-fed. Oh, you got this lead system." There's always an excuse, right? Then, we feel bad. "Oh, you got a lay down sale. That wasn't a sell. You didn't close them. Dude, that was a lay down." We start thinking we don't deserve shit. This is our society in the sales world, especially if we have a good month, and our manager discounts us.

Ladies, don't shoot me down. The way to score a hot chick is to do differently than every other guy does. Every other guy is all up her ass, drooling all over, offering her diamonds right off the date, or right off the jump. The key to scoring a hot chick is to be indifferent. Don't be like every other dude who's approached her. The reason why I say this is you've got to be different when you approach. With sales, it's the same thing. It's like we're the same way. We're like the hot chicks, right? The sales manager talks negatively to us. "Hey, I just closed 50 deals this month." "That's great, you loser. If you are any kind of a winner, you'll close a hundred." It's the same thing they do to us. We want what we can't have, and somebody to be like, "Attaboy! Great job." Most of us wouldn't be encouraged by that. Most of us will try twice as hard to prove somebody is wrong than we will to prove somebody right.

Why don't you think you deserve it? What is that? There's an anchor somewhere. When Adam and I were talking, he said, "Man, you know, it took me a long time to get to 90 grand, and I'd go blow $20,000 on direct response mail, or some shit that I knew may not work that well. I knew I needed to save that money up. Finally, I did these slips, and I got this money now." He was like, "Man, that's just there. I might as well deal with it." The reason why I say that; it's not about the money. I'm not bragging on Adam's behalf or talking about money in my bank account or anything like that, but I know that a lot of people suffering from upper limits see it in their bank account.

A guy on Facebook the other day said, "I just inherited

$25,000. What should I do with it?" I told him exactly what to do with it in terms of real estate, leverage in the bank, doing the right thing with his money, but I also told him about upper limits. I said, "You know you just got this money. You're trying to throw it right away. Could you imagine if you worked your entire life, 29 years, 40 hours a week every week, and this was your life savings? Would you just want to give it away that fast?" This was his upper limit. He'd never had anything like that before. He was uncomfortable as fuck with it. He didn't get it out of his bank account. I know a lot of people are the same way. That's why you're ready to learn about making a change.

You get to a point where you're uncomfortable even though that point should make you more comfortable, right? You should be more comfortable with that money in your bank account because that money represents security. Instead, we get scared because we don't think we deserve it. That's some deeply rooted psychological shit that doesn't have anything to do with the money. It doesn't have anything to do with the fact that you keep getting drunk, going and spending your money on Amazon, or the fact that you keep going out when you know you need to save money. You're buying shit that's way out of your price range, that you shouldn't have been messing with in the first place, but you get uncomfortable when you live right when you put money in that bank account. You get uncomfortable when you look up, and you see investments that you've made and the portfolio that you've built because most of us grew up poor. We don't feel like we deserve this shit because we've been under mass hypnosis from the government, the media, the Internet and all these other places for all these years.

They've led us into these upper limits. But we know they have a root, and that they came from somewhere. I challenge you to write down where these upper limits originated. We're going to identify them in a minute. But ask yourself: *Where have these upper limits originated from?* What instances in your life bring these things up? Look, it's time that you just get comfortable being who you are, that you are comfortable earning what you believe you've got coming to you, that you feel good about deserving something. We have upper limits because we feel like we don't deserve them. Well, oftentimes, we feel like we haven't earned them. Take, for example, the guy that messaged me on Facebook with the $25,000. If he had earned that $25,000 and logically saved it over the course of 10 years, he would feel like, he what? He deserved it.

Since he got it in one lump sum, the issue was he didn't feel like he'd earned it. He didn't feel like he deserved it. Here's the thing. If you're trusted with it, if life gives you a chance to where you're handed money, if you earned a good commission check, if you make a good settlement, if something happens and you're trusted with money, that's life going, "Let's see what the fuck you got." Guess what? Life's throwing a Hail Mary, and what do they do? They fumble this son of a bitch and drop it out of bounds and lose the damn game of life. We've seen it happen. Life's throwing you a Hail Mary right into your fingertips, and you're running at the perfect speed, running the line with it. For some reason, you swat the damn thing out of bounds.

You know why? Because you feel like you don't deserve it. Life's giving it to you. Life's saying, "Hey, you deserve this." You're going, "Oh, shit. No, I don't." You're arguing with the universe. Now, I'm not here to share some hokey, universal and spiritual law of attraction, but dude, I'm telling you. If it came to you, you attracted it. If you deflected it, that was your own doing. The universe was saying, "You've done the job to take this money. You've done the job to have this in your savings. You've done the job to earn this commission check. You've done the job to have this pipeline. You've done the job to get this promotion, to have this girl and everything else that's involved." If you don't take it, then, you're deflecting it.

Man, we see Johnny Manziel. He's the greatest example right now of someone who hit the upper limits. Rich family but changed the way A&M football was played and stadium tickets were sold and just changed the game for them. Came up to the Cleveland Browns. I think that's who he plays for. Maybe the Bengals. It doesn't matter. When he came up, there was going to be this savior to take their team to the Super Bowl. Here, we have Tim Tebow, right? He's the guy that everybody felt was the awesomest dude ever, was going to be great. He didn't really do much in the NFL. Then, Johnny Football was supposed to be that guy. He was the guy in college and the guy in the NFL. He was supposed to have everything. What happened? He hit upper limits. You can find Johnny in a bar, drinking, just spending. He's probably got a little bit of money. He's the sports' world's biggest letdown right now.

Jon Jones, another guy, a title, supposed to fight last night. For some reason, he decided to do shit that he knew he shouldn't have done that would have got him kicked out because he felt like he didn't deserve it. He has been on performance-enhancing drugs and knew that he didn't earn it. He caved with his mass hypnosis because of the phrases I mentioned. Money is the root of all evil. You win the lottery. You spend your money. We're under all this mass hypnosis, and I want you to start identifying these upper limits when they happen to you. The first way to do that is if it's a money upper limit, set the bar low. Get comfortable having $2,000 or $3,000 in your bank account. Save up to it. If you have no money right now, that's fine. Save up to $2,000 or $3,000 and leave it there. Get used to it.

Back in 2004, I had never had any money before. I had a house that I bought. We got foreclosed on. Every dollar that I made in the mortgage business, I spent on drugs and partying and my truck and some shit, right, because I had never had any money before. I didn't have anybody teach me how to use it. I felt money was the root of all evil. I was trying to make money buy me happiness instead of money saving me or investing me into happiness. I'd make nine grand in a month, and then be the brokest son of a bitch on the block. I had seen guys in the sales world do this all the time. They have $25,000-$30,000 paychecks. Not months, not weeks… Paychecks, then they blow it off. People come to me. They say, "Hey, man. I just made a $200,000 commission check. I need to buy a portion of the house quick. I need to do something with it."

I just got paid last week, but here I am, spending it all. It has taken me my entire life to get this check, but here I am, trying to spend it all in one swoop. People know that they have a big check coming on the way. What do they start doing? They start planning what they're going to spend it on. Now, listen. I'm not here to tell you to save your money, but oftentimes, what happens is that people who are planning on spending that money are not doing it in investments. They're using it on dumb shit, right? I'm not asking you to save money. What I am asking you to do is to get comfortable having a certain amount of money in your account.

Right now, if you're broke, you need to save up your first thousand dollars and take a deep breath. Get comfortable with having a grand in there. Then, you know what? Push through that upper limit and say, "You know what? I'm going to get comfortable having three." Save your money. Put your money back. Now, you got $3,000 in your bank account. Guess what the next move is? Five, right? That's only logical. "Guess I worked for it. I earned it. I saved it. I can breathe. I can feel it. I'm OK with it. I'm getting comfortable. I'm at one with the bank account balance," and you continue to go through that path. "I deserve this. I earned it."

You see, I have this system that I follow as religiously as I can. If I want something, I save up enough money to go get it, but I don't buy it until I have the money. Oftentimes, what happens is once I've saved up the money that it took for me to get something, because I have the same damn upper limits, too, I go to get it, and I realize that's not what I want. A few weeks ago, I was going to get this fancy race car. It's like a $250,000 race car. It's going to be awesome. It took $25,000 above and beyond what I was already spending on my bills and everything else to be able to afford this race car. Then, I had to put a significant amount of money down.

I thought I could sell it at the end and profit from it. It would be awesome. Maybe not profit, but at least break even for driving this awesome McLaren for the time. I took a few weeks. I shit you not, saved up the $25,000 it was going to take to get started on the process with the car. Had an exit strategy where I can make $25,000 on the backend even if I just paid the monthly on the car. Maybe I could make a little profit if I didn't put that many miles on it. After I put the plan and money together, the dealership called us. I said, "I'm going to skip this one because I found an investment somewhere else that would pay me more money. That got my attention." Sure, I didn't get the gratification of having the McLaren right that minute, but I found an investment that will make me enough money to where I'll be able to buy five of them by the time it's over with. It's not a big deal. It's just delayed gratification.

However, what if I had just been in the position that I already had the money? I wanted to save that 25 grand above and beyond what I already have. Here's why: Because I wanted to feel like I earned it and deserved it. I didn't want it to be an upper limit reason as to why I'm buying this McLaren. Guess what? I think it was. Instead, I found some investments to invest in. Well, for sure, it's delayed gratification, but here's what I've learned, and this is the reason why I've been doing this for the last 10 years. When I have something that I want, I don't buy it immediately. I save the money that it takes for me to buy the thing. Then, I make the logical, emotion-free decision. If I want something really bad and I've worked for it, and I have the money, and I've saved the money, and I still want it, then I just buy it.

By the time I'd saved this money, it just took a couple of weeks. I'm fortunate enough to where I can make a lot of sales. It just took me a couple of weeks to go out here and put together the money. By the time I had it, there was something else that I was onto that made me feel better. Guess what? I started the process again. Let me save the money to get this thing. Let's see if I still feel the same way about it. I do.

How many times have you had this happen? Somebody hits you up with a deal. Then you're like, "Fuck, man. If I wouldn't have spent that money last week. Fuck, man. If I'd just hung onto that check." My boy hits me up out of Florida a month and a half ago. He says, "Hey, man. If you got cash, this is the deal of the century; $120,000, it can be yours. You sell it for $170,000." He went bullshit, and we got it for $115,000. We have it listed right now for $160,000, and it's below the market price. We'll probably get in a bad situation, which is exciting for me. Guess what? If I would have had those upper limits, if I wouldn't have had the money, I wouldn't have been able to jump on that opportunity. How many times has somebody called you and said, "Hey, man. I know that you just got that big check from XYZ. Let's do this." You're like, "I already spent it." "On what?" "Bubblegum and baseball cards."

Remember as a little kid? Your grandpa gives you five dollars, ten dollars. You didn't keep the money and put it in your piggy bank, did you? What did you do? You went and bought bubblegum and baseball cards. It's the same shit you do as an adult. Same pattern, nothing's changed. It's just, instead of bubblegum and baseball cards, it's just some dumb shit from Amazon and pants from North Face when you know you shouldn't have spent that 200 bucks. You should have saved it. It's the latest fucking iPhone. All right, I know some people in my life, and they have the fanciest damn phone on the planet, and they have one of the shittiest paying jobs you'd ever know. That's an upper limit. That's hypnosis.

Let's identify these patterns in your life. There's the money piece? If you have no money, just save up your first grand. Get used to it. Feel like you deserve it. Move on. What about the relationship side of things? It's like what we watch in every movie. The dude finally gets the girl, and then he does something to try to push her away. The chick finally gets the dude of her dreams, and she does something to push him away. That's the classic Hollywood example of an upper limit. You finally found the person of your dreams, but you're a complete asshole to him. You finally found the person of your dreams, but you're like, "I don't know because I'm with Steve over here," right? "I don't know because I'm with some mediocre person," right? We've all seen the movies, and we know people who are way talented individuals, but their significant other is a turd. They hit an upper limit. That's who they think they deserve. Their low self-esteem comes into play.

What pattern, right? In the past, you've been in a perfect relationship before. You've blown it. How? Where have you repeated that because how you do anything, is how you do everything, right? Where are you blowing things? Where are you repeating this process? At work, you get the dream job. You get to the top. I have salespeople all the time. They're like, "Hey, I'm the top producer in my field. I'm looking to switch fields." What the fuck for? You're the top producer. Expand that shit. What do you want to stop for? "Oh, it's not challenging anymore." Challenge yourself.

See, what happens is that build and destroy, that same process applies. "Oh, I've been top producer in five different fields." What the fuck for, man? Why are you not top producer across the board in that field? One of those upper limits, the build and destroy hits. Start identifying that in your life. What are your patterns? Things start going well. What do you do to destroy them? *Hey, I know things are going good for me.* I start fights like a drunk guy. The guy who's had enough to drink. You want to fight everybody. It shows his true colors. He's having too much of a good time. He wants to fight it. I'm the same way, right? Things are getting in place for me. I want to start some shit with somebody. Somebody call me a piece of shit because I feel like I need to be called that every now and then; it's just an ego check, and I do it subconsciously. I catch myself. I say, "Dammit, Ryan. What the hell are you arguing with this idiot for?"

I bet you do the same thing. You might quit your job, or yell at your spouse. That's another one. We get mad at our significant others. For what? For some bullshit oftentimes. The things that we could have just been better off getting along with and saving face and not being all that. Make-up sex may be one thing, but at the same time, we'll fight with our significant others for no apparent reason. Things get going too good in the house. We have to have some drama because that's what we're used to. We can't have a two-year-long happiness streak. There's got to be some sort of fight around here. That's normal. That's what our parents did. That's what our grandparents did. That's what people on TV do. We've got to make sure that we do that as well, right?

Screaming at your kids, you know? Things go well. You kick your dog. You're screaming at your kids. They can be doing their thing and being awesome, and we find ways to get them out of it. We have the most loving kids ever, and we could be totally mean to them. I see people all the time with their kids coming to them, telling them how much they love them. That's upper limits. That's because they don't want to receive the love from their kids because they don't feel like they're worthy of that love. When they're doing actions like pushing the kid away from them, they're really not.

Let me tell you. Amy's been gone for a week. Jackson and I

have been hanging out. I haven't taken him to school since last Monday. Oh, fuck it. I pay for it. It doesn't matter. Jackson and I have been to the park every day, at least one park. We've been to the pool every other day. We spent four hours today, me, teaching him how to swim. We ride the bikes every night. We race in hoverboards. We ride in motorcycles. We go into Dave and Buster's. We've been to a few other places as well. The reason why I say all this is because I've fed him every meal, and I still work a job. I didn't take this week off. I've been able to do this and still work this week. You get on the happiness factor like that, and there's got to be some reason for you to want to destroy that relationship with your kids, but we do all this stuff because we have no upper limits.

We enjoy our time, and I make sure that, "Hey, there's no need to destroy this and find a reason." Your parents are always like, "I'll turn this car around. I'll go home. I'll turn this car around." There's no reason for us to do that.

Think about these identifying factors in your life. Things that started happening. Things that go well, and what do you do, you get up to where things are good. You get up to where you're making money. What are your spending habits? What are your saving habits? What are your investing habits? You get the perfect chick again, finally. How do you screw it up? You cheated on her. You're mean to her. You don't listen to her. You push her away. Same with the dudes. Quit the job; get the dream job; get the dream commission plan. I'm asking you to identify. We've explored where it comes from, why it's there and what it's doing in your life. The logical next phase would be like, "OK, so what do you do to push through it?"

Well, here's the thing, Now, you're aware. Once you're aware of things, it's like before you were ignorant, you don't know you didn't know. Now, you're aware. Now you know. First of all, when you become conscious of something, and you're aware of something, guess what that also does? That removes your excuses. From this point on, if you hit upper limits, it's your fault. There is no excuse for it. You're aware of it. You're conscious of it. You know about it. You've been educated about it. It's important that you understand that these upper limits exist and that you look for them. Be aware of them to show up in your life.

Expect them to show up and be aware. It's a neighborhood alert to be on the lookout for a burglar; you will be aware at night. You'll sleep a little bit lighter. You damn sure wouldn't go to sleep with a blindfold and earplugs. You'd sleep with one eye open, gripping your pillow tight.

Here's the other thing, and I'm working on this for my permission-based selling program. I'm making sales affirmations. It's important that you affirm yourself daily. When I was going through the time of my life when I was running through upper limits with money, I looked myself in the mirror and said, "You are worth $100,000. You are worth $10,000. You have earned this."

"You are worth it. You have earned it." I told myself action statements, affirmations.

Action statements and affirmations to ensure my subconscious because guess what? My entire life, I have been programmed that money was the root of all evil. You know what I mean? Easy come. Easy go. I had to unprogram myself, and the only way to remove and fill up old data, old space, is with new data and new space. It's garbage in, garbage out. The only way I could push the old stuff out was to fill my head with new stuff. Amy and I, listen to this hour-long affirmation thing on YouTube when we go to sleep, which is actually eight hours long.

Affirm yourself because you do deserve to win. You have put in the time. You are at this moment in your life or in the future moment of your life. Identify patterns that keep showing up.

Here's what I recommend, especially when it comes to business. You can't really do this in your family life, but this is huge when it comes to business. Oftentimes, what will happen is we'll build a business up to a certain degree, a certain level, a certain limit. Then, we'll start looking for reasons to shut it down, sell it, not take interest in it anymore. It's almost like having sex with somebody after the first date. It might have been the most remarkable person ever, but you know what? You got everything you wanted out of it on the first date. There's nothing left to conceal there, right? It's just how it works. It's human nature.

In business, instead of hitting upper limits, instead of tearing things down to start all over, what I recommend is firing yourself from positions. I fired myself from the sales position and made myself CEO. I fired myself from funnel-maker. I trained Pat, put him in there and then fired myself from making funnels anymore. I fired myself from those roles that would allow me to have upper limits. Right now, there are four people in management in my company: Amy, Roxanne, Lindsay and Pat. Those four people allow me not to have those limits. Roxanne could tell you plenty of times. I'm like, "Shut it down. Fucking fire all the sales team. Fuck this shit, motherfucker. It's fucking over with. I'm done with all of them." She's like, "OK, sure. I got you, boss." She just goes on about her day. She knows that's my upper limit.

Same thing with Amy. I could be like, "Hey, you know what? Fuck that. Yes, we're not going to do that." She's like, "Hey, Ryan, they love it. I'll deal with it," because she knows I'm hitting my upper limits. I have other people in my life aware for me and of me as well. That's your thing. You have to build a team around you if you're going through business, and you've torn up businesses in the past. You've been destructive of something you've built in the past. You know this is your upper limit, what you have identified as one of your problems. So, the thing that you have to do is build this thing up and fire yourself as fast as possible. That's an old Richard Branson saying, right?

He doesn't want to run all these companies. He doesn't know what's going on in every one of his companies. What he's done is fired himself from every position along the way to where his responsibility is less and less. Not that he's like some great business god, which he obviously is at this point, but it's this philosophy that got him there. It's so he can't fuck it up. He put somebody in place without those upper limits. Most of us salespeople are damaged fucking goods. We have a lot of upper limits. We'll have great ideas and massive-ass execution, but then, we'll have upper limits to go along with them.

A lot of times, the Harolds don't. A visionary like Richard Branson needs somebody with a Harvard degree and some Harold in HR with engineering ingenuity on the backend to run the ship for him. He can dream it up, but he knows his upper limits. "Hey, it's not worth it. Get rid of it." I think about Clyxo all the time. "What if I just sold it?" I don't want to be like the dude that sold Victoria's Secret for a million bucks. It's a billion-dollar-a-year company now, multi-billion-dollar. Here's the thing. Build it for yourself but inform others. Let your spouse know your upper limit patterns. I tell Amy all the time "I don't feel like I deserve you, so when you see me fighting with you, just tell me how much you love me." It makes me feel good. That's my upper limit. What's yours?

Let's look for each other's upper limits and be aware for each other. Here's the crazy thing. It's easier for you to point out the speck in my eye than the plank in your own. So, if you're looking out for others and they're looking out for you, and your heart has the best of intentions, then there's a chance you can break a person from hitting that upper limit or help them at least push through it. Listen, if two of you get together and start pushing through the limits, then there shouldn't be any upper limits. There shouldn't be a limit at all. If you don't have a spouse, a friend, a business partner, or somebody else can help you out with this. You can say, "I have the tendency to do this." A gentleman and I right now, are partnered up on a real estate firm. Dude's one of the hardest working guys I know. He's built his firm up from nothing. He's killing it.

We have a conversation. He's like, "Here's my tendency to where I fuck things up. I need you to help me." I've seen a conversation where: "Here's the shit that I don't like doing and I get mad over, and I fuck things up." We have this conversation up front because we can hold each other accountable. More importantly, we know it in order to recognize each other's patterns. "Remember that conversation we had before we got started? I think that's happening right now." Listen, it may be a moment of vulnerability for us that we may have become aware of. I mean, to some of us, our ego may think that makes us look weak, but really, it makes you strong. Because a strong leader knows his weaknesses and isn't afraid to point them out to people who lack those weaknesses and instead have strengths in those areas. A strong leader should be able to delegate.

I'd like to tell you now that there's just never going to be an upper limit in your life again if you push through that shit.

Upper limits are some real shit. There's going to be some people who go get an accountability partner after being exposed to them. Then tell your business partner or your spouse, just let them know how you're feeling and how you're rolling. Just be brutally honest with them. Other people will respond differently to this subject. "I don't have upper limits," and then you wonder why you keep riding this roller coaster. Maybe it's like some of you that do have a big commission month, and then you have two or three shitty commission months where you don't hardly make anything. You have a big commission month again. You have two or three shitty commission months. That's another sign of upper limits, the roller coaster of commissions.

Here's what you can do. When you realize you're hitting your upper limits, when you realize you're going into a pattern, the thing that you can't do is you can't breathe, right? When your bank account gets five grand, ten grand, a hundred grand, whatever that uncomfortable number for you is, a million bucks, whatever. When you feel that, and you get there, and you have the tendency to want to spend it all or blow it all or do some dumb shit, breathe. Take it in. Feel it. Feel it inside you. Take it in. Get comfortable with it. When we go on stage to speak in front of people—which public speaking is the number one fear in America—the thing that we do is we just take a deep breath. Start taking it all in and go with it. We're going to jump off a cliff. What's the first thing that we do? Take it all in. Take a deep breath. Get comfortable with it. If we're going to go in for the kiss, if we're going to go out, ask for the date, we're going to ask for the business, "Here goes nothing." You're breathing in your situation. Same thing.

I remember when I first broke through that 6-figure number in my bank account. I had six figures laying around in my bank account. I have more than that now. I remember the first time. I was like, "Fuck, man. Take that in. You made it here." It's like, "Dude. You saved this much money up, man. You did it. What should we invest in? How can we get here faster? How can we stop blowing money on dumb shit and get here faster?" How can we stop screwing up relationships and get what we want? How can we stop fucking over good jobs that we have and stop fucking over good friends that we have? How can we stop doing this?" I have all these issues, myself, right? I'm not immune from any of these, but I identify myself now, and in most cases, stop myself from letting these upper limits really put in any mainline restrictions on me.

Here's the homework I recommend. Identify the root where it all started for you. What patterns showed up early on in your life? Phrases, things of that nature. Money is the root of all evil. Money can't buy you love. What phrases? What are all these identifiers? Then, next step. Identify why you're letting them affect you. Why do they exist? Why do you let them affect you? Why don't you think you deserve it? Then, identify your patterns. "Here's the default mode that I go into. Things get going great, and I do X, Y, Z." "I get this amount of money saved up, and I do X, Y, Z." Then, share that with somebody close to you. Somebody who most likely won't hurt you. Somebody maybe you've known for a long time that's seen you do this before and will be actually glad to hear you admit it and help you through it. You'd be surprised.

There are no more excuses. You're aware of the upper limits. You're aware of how to identify them, where they come from, the reason they exist and how to move forward from them. My intention is for you to be great, for you to do more than you're doing right now and for people to look back one day and say, "That person changed lives." If you keep doing the same old patterns, running the same old bullshit upper limits, you're never going to get there. You deserve what you've got coming to you. The lay downs, the big commission checks. That's the universe saying, "Hey, you've done the work. You deserve this." You blowing it, spending it, giving it back, is you saying, "No, I don't." Listen, the universe's infinite wisdom is way smarter than any of us are. Let go of those upper limits, yo.

Now that you're aware, now that you know that these patterns exist in your life do all you can to avoid them. That's what we deserve. If we're going to be great, we're going to do great things for great people, raise up future leaders and all these other visions we have for ourselves, we can, at least, feel like we earned this stuff, and at least, do good with what we're handed.

Chapter #6: Relationships

Relationships, I'm definitely not an expert. I'm just going to give you real world personal experiences and share with you the lessons that you can learn from them.

Last night, one of the guys in the sales group mentioned he's having some problems with his wife. I thought *I can give some insights into some ways that I fucked a lot of stuff up, honestly, some ways that you can avoid making the mistakes that I did.* I think that there are two ways to learn. There's: you learn from your own mistakes, or you can learn from somebody else's mistakes.

Oftentimes, if we don't make a mistake, we don't receive the correction. When you don't receive correction, you don't receive direction. We don't really know where we're going. Think about it: When you're in school, the teacher asks you what two plus two is, and you say a number. You make a mistake; she corrects you. That's how you learn. You do long division, or you're writing your English papers. You do the things that you learn because the teacher's pointing out your mistakes. I remember you could get graded and make five or 10 mistakes and fail the entire page in school. That might only be, shit, 5 or 10 words out of 100 words that you wrote for example. But those teachers would always point the mistakes out to you.

I believe fully that I am in the position that I am in because of the mistakes that I've made and the ability to endure them. How to get through the bullshit, that's what the bottom line is. How to deal with life, how to get the most from life and get through the bullshit. The bullshit doesn't have to be sad or depressing. The bullshit can often be what you don't need to be doing. You want to know to get out, how to step into a CEO role. Over here at Hardcore Closer a year and a half ago that's what happened. I wasn't going to advance as a salesperson; I had to step into a CEO role. I had to get away from some of the bullshit.

I'm not talking about relationships in the sense of who you're banging right now either. That's part of it, but that's not the gist of it. We have relationships with our kids, our grandparents, our friends, our co-workers, the staff that works for us, the executives that we work for, the customers that we work for, the contractors that work for us. We have relationships with everybody.

Here's the thing, and I'll say it again: How you do anything is how you do everything. If you're screwing up at home, you're probably screwing up at work, too. The difference is your wife, or your husband will tell you where you're screwing up and fight back. Your employees don't want to lose their jobs, so they just keep their lips sealed. Then you're wondering why you're losing money or you're wondering why things aren't going as well. You're wondering why your team is not selling as well as they should or not being as productive as they should. A lot of times, in our world, the sales world, we sell a lot of stuff, then we have the people behind the scenes that have to do the delivery and the other jobs for us, and they might be slow.

Prepare yourself. Think about this once more. How you do anything is how you do everything. Everything we'll cover here applies not just to relationships. Even if I'm using the specific example of a relationship, that doesn't mean that it stops there. It applies in every relationship. I don't mean just the person that you're banging, not just your husband, your wife, your boyfriend, your girlfriend, your fiancé; this applies to everybody you work with.

Chances are, you may not see it. Oftentimes, if people don't tell us shit, we think we're fine. We're graded in life by our mistakes. If people aren't willing to point out our mistakes, then how will we learn? The problem is so many of us don't want to learn. We say we want to learn, but we don't want to learn because if someone pointed out our mistakes, we'd get mad and snap at them. We get defensive.

Part one involves an alignment. I'm not talking about cars. I'm talking about who you surround yourself with, who you hang out with, who you do life with. That's your alignment. I used to go to this church in Frisco, Texas. The preacher man is one of the coldest salespeople I've ever seen in my life. He used to always say these catchy phrases. He probably still does. I don't know. I don't watch him anymore. He would say, "Alignment takes precedence over assignment." I thought, shit, that's a really strong thing. I'm stealing it from him. I'm sure he stole it from somebody else, too. That's how the whole word game works.

The alignment taking precedence over assignment to me means who you do life with is more important than what you do in life. Here's why, because who you do life with can also dictate what you do in life. If you hang around a bunch of millionaires, then you're able to raise the capital for the right investment, get advised on the right level and be able to do big things. If you're hanging around a bunch of bonehead thugs, that's what my stepdad used to always call them, if you hang around a bunch of bonehead thugs, you end up like me, in prison.

I've spent a long time thinking about all of this. Not just since the preacher told it to me the first time in 2004 either. It was a bad time in life. I had gotten in with the wrong people; I was on drugs and didn't have my shit together. I can look back to that point right there, and I can say everything that happened to me was because of who was around me. Not because it was their fault. Most of it was my fault. Some of us were co-conspirators. I remember thinking *it's because of this chain of events, that this occurred*. I know that if I hadn't been aligned with those people, the things that had taken place wouldn't have happened.

I know if I wouldn't have made the alignments that I made in the drug game that I wouldn't have gone to prison. I know if I hadn't worked in the car wash, I wouldn't have ever met the main drug dealer guy. I know that if I wouldn't have had these friends...and on it goes. Some of us always try to be these heroes. We have friends on drugs. We don't do drugs, but we still try to look out for them. We hope they get their life together, but we're not bold enough to say anything to them because they're on drugs and they might say something crazy to us.

Maybe you're going, "Yeah, man, my brother's that way. Yeah man, my best friend's that way. My wife hates him when he comes over all the time high as fuck. He's my boy. We've known each other for a long time." That's alignment. Much like a car, when you're out of alignment, your shit steers off the path, or it becomes more difficult to guide in the path that you want to go. Alignments aka relationships, some of the questions I'll ask you are going to be difficult. Some of it's going to be hard.

I'll tell you my story and the examples and the lessons along the way. You're going to have to ask yourself a lot of these same questions I've had to ask myself. There are two things happening to us at all times. We're running through this game of life. We've got people holding our hands that are running, trying to pull us with them, trying to make us go faster. We've got people that have got our hand, and they're trying to pull us back to them, running backwards. It's our job to continue running. It's always about perpetual motion.

There are two types of people out there. It's rare that you see people that are able to go hand in hand. I was with Mike Reese and Jay Kinder this morning for breakfast. We ate breakfast at about 7 a.m. Those guys are rare examples of people who have had a partnership for 10 years. I've seen a lot of people in the business world have partnership after partnership. I've seen Jay and Mike together forever, and it's rare to find somebody who will pull their own weight. Sometimes, you're the dead weight. I've been the dead weight before, too. It gets hard to get other people to pull their weight. It frustrates you. So, that's why we need to dissect this alignment thing.

I'm just going to throw this number out there. From personal experiences and listening to people's messages over the years. When I say listening to people's message over the years, I'm talking about thousands of Facebook messages through my fan page from people who have had relationship alignment problems with their work, with their spouse, their kids, etc. About eight out of 10 things that you have relationships with right now just need to go; this is 80 percent—the 80-20 rule. The 80 percent of the relationships you have right now are holding you back. You know why? Because 80 percent of the world is, you could say average. They say, "That would be 50 percent, Ryan," but 80 percent of the world is really average. They're surely not supernatural. They're surely not energy producers. Eighty percent of the world is the "blah" crowd.

We see ourselves as performers; we like to think that we're the 20 percent, the one percent. We're the ones who fucking do what we say we're going to do; we fucking do it when we say we're going to do it. We're the ones who follow through; we're the ones who pull our weight; we're the ones who do what's right. We don't have to fucking do shady shit. Those are all the things that we do. There's not that many of us. You say, "Dude, Ryan, you're a breath of fresh air. You keep it real. There's nobody else like that." No shit, because at least 80 percent of the motherfuckers around on this planet are just fucking dust in the wind, like a cancer. They're just aimlessly wandering through life. God bless them. I'm not mad at them. I don't hate them. I'm just saying that the fucking numbers don't lie. You can see it.

Because of those numbers, your numbers in the friend world aren't any different. That means that 80 percent of the people in your life most likely have to go. Man, it's fucking difficult losing people that you love. Oftentimes, you have to ask yourself when you're in alignment with something you love, your work, your spouse, your relationship with your significant other if you're not happy. On the surface, you feel like you've got it all under control. You're in this alignment, and you've made a decision somewhere along the way that you're going to stay in the alignment.

Have you had a business partner who didn't do what they said they were going to do? You went into a business venture; you threw money in it, you threw time in it, sweat equity, the whole nine, and your business partner didn't do what the fuck they said they were going to do. We've all fucking been there. Have you had a girlfriend or boyfriend who said they were going to do some shit? They said they were going to be there for you, and then when the shit hit the fan, they fucking weren't?

Have you taken those fucking partners back? Have you let those significant others get away with it? Time and time again. There's this thing called the click-whirr method. If you read the book *Influence* by Dr. Robert Cialdini, it's one of the greatest sales books ever written. In this book, *Influence* by Dr. Cialdini, he talks about something called the click-whirr method. He talks about how usually only sociopaths won't go back on their word. We hear these things like opposites attract and other sayings. They are complete bullshit. I'm going to get real with you now. I'll explain. This click-whirr is what keeps us in the relationship. It's our monkey brain taking over because we're all primates. It's our primate brain taking over; it's the old part, the archaic part of our brain taking over. We're still driven by that in one form or another.

I read this the other day from a monk. And what you've got to do is great. You've got to tell your monkey brain what to do. You've got to control it. You've got to give it instructions. When they're trying to do meditation, you don't have to lock yourself in a box and be an enlightened douchebag or any of that stuff. All you have to do is tell your brain to follow your breath. You have to give the brain something to do. Follow your breath, over and over again. Follow your breath, over and over again. He explains that we're giving tasks to our monkey brain so that we can get clarity. Small, easy tasks.

The reason why I say that, is we have this monkey brain. It works in certain ways. You've got psychological hacks for instance.

There's even a drug out there, scopolamine. You can take it in Columbia, and people will control your brain. When you take this shit, the next thing you know, somebody can be like, "Give me all your money and your furniture." You'll help them move it out. Happy as hell. "Take my furniture, Fernando, appreciate it." Crazy as hell. It's a beautiful tree, too, just like everything else in Columbia, beautiful and deadly.

Because of this click-whirr method, we stick with the people that we need to ditch. If you've made an agreement with somebody, the click-whirr method is what keeps you from breaking that agreement. In sales, if I can get you to agree to something and later on when you give me an objection, I can say, "But didn't you already agree to do this?" We'll keep moving forward. We've agreed to take these relationships on. We agreed with the boss and the owner of the company that we sell stuff or work for them. We agreed with that business partner that we would sell goods. We have an agreement with them.

Most of us, especially the type of people I'm used to working with, don't like to go back on their words. They say give an inch, take a mile, but if you give somebody a little leeway with their word, they'll get worse and worse. This is what happens with relationships. We think we can get the person to show up the way we want. All the business partners not showing up right now. All the spouses not showing up right now. They're not doing what they're supposed to do. They're not holding up their end of the agreement. We remember there was a time when they did hold up their end of the agreement, and we think we can get back there.

You get focused on getting them back to how things were in the beginning, and they're focused on escalating things the way that they are now. You're on two different paths that are out of alignment. Sometimes it goes slow. Sometimes people stay married for 10 or 15 years before the alignment is finally so out of whack that you can't drive the car together anymore. We make these decisions. Just like when you get a dog. You ever see somebody with a fucking ugly dog? They made the decision to pick the dog up, and the dog was their puppy, and they grew up with it, and it gets older, and the dog is fucking ugly. Ugly. You ever seen that? They made the decision, they made the agreement, that that dog was theirs no matter what.

When you marry somebody, that's what you're saying. No matter what, we're going to get married and stay married forever. If you go to work for somebody, it's like, "No matter what, I'm going to work here for the rest of my life. No matter what, I'm going to be a part of this partnership for the rest of my life." Whether it is business or otherwise. Because of that, we stick with people that we need to ditch. Family included. Family especially. It's not easy.

I had a guy reach out to me this morning. His brother committed his third or fourth felony. He'd gotten pulled over again last night, and then some more trouble ensued. The family wants him to go get his brother out because he got his brother out last time. The whole family is mad at him. He's saying, "He didn't learn his lesson. I'm not getting him out." The whole family is mad at him because he won't go get him out. Where's the family? These are the kinds of relationships that happen. Where's the family in this? None of them are going to get the guy out. They put it back on my friend who feels all this pressure in the world because of his alignments. He needs to get rid of about 80 percent of those people.

It's sad. I'm in a position right now where I don't talk to my grandparents. My 4-year-old son wants to know where they're at. I don't talk to my parents. None of them. I talk to my brother every now and then. One of my sisters is in Korea. She's chilling. I don't know what the fuck happened there. She just wanted to probably get away from all this bullshit. My brother is in the National Guard. I talk to him pretty regularly. My other sister, I haven't talked to her in years. Since right around the time Jax was born when I stopped talking to my mom and stepdad.

Here's why I share that with you. When I let go of my parents, it was the final string for me. Your parents, they always say these things, "We raised you. We wiped your ass when you were a kid. We know everything about you." I always felt like my parents were blackmailing me. They would give me this sob story so that I would do things for them. I started making money. I'm not saying they weren't making money, but as I started making six figures a year, they wanted to get in on more and more shit that I did. It seemed like they always had me in some fucking bullshit. At the time, as a kid, I looked at it, and I thought *this is just normal family shit*.

People who say family sticks together and gets through shit…they are the people who need family. We do need family, but there's two kinds of family. There's the family of origin, who birthed you, and there's the family of choice. Oftentimes, we keep relationships with the family of origin when it's time to let them go. When the young male lion comes of age, he doesn't hang out with his mom anymore. He goes out and creates another pride of female lions and starts to carry on a legacy. If he has a son, the son goes off, and so on and so forth.

We, as humans, who are supposed to be the most evolved on the planet, stick with our family no matter what. We're one of the only ones in the animal kingdom that doesn't send our males off. If you're a lion and you get to where you're two years old, and you're hanging out in the pride, the other male lions like your dad, will say, "Yo, you gots to go, man. You got to get your own food. You can't hang out here anymore." We do this for 18 years before our parents say, "You're on your own. You got to go get your own food now." But then, thanks to technology and everything else, cars, transportation, we stay in touch with each other, unlike animals in the animal kingdom.

Staying in touch with each other oftentimes causes pressure. We think we love people in our family, or we think we love a specific person, but your friends will tell you you're fucking crazy to go through this. Why are you putting yourself through this pain? Because outsiders can see it from a logical standpoint. When you're in the relationship and in the agreement, the click-whirr from your monkey brain keeps you addicted to the peptides. This is all a chemical action here. It keeps you addicted to the peptides that your brain pumps from honoring that agreement being with that person. You can get that same peptide with the right people. The problem is, how are you ever going to find the right person to have the relationship with or the right company to have a relationship with or the right business partner to have the relationship with if you don't dump the fucking shitty ones you have right now?

Let's talk about doing that. Early on, I introduced the idea that alignment takes precedence over assignment. Remember that? Now, I'm going to share with you about assignments. Have you thought about really what it is that you're supposed to do? The reason why I ask is there's a voice at the back of each one of our heads guiding us, telling us what we're supposed to do. I had a relationship with a bank. I loved it. It was exactly what I wanted to be doing at that time of my life. The government passed the Dodd-Frank Act, and I lost my license and ultimately that relationship with the bank. I had to go out on my own.

I wasn't listening to the voice. The voice never told me to be a banker. Yes, that was part of my path, but I fell in love with something that should have been a one-night stand. Track with me now. We have an assignment. There is a divine assignment on us. There is something out there in the universe that says, "This person is born for this reason." Most of us spend the rest of our fucking entire life avoiding that reason. When we avoid that reason, we're not being who we are because that voice is telling us who we're supposed to be. That voice is assigning us to what we're supposed to do on this planet. What happens? We ignore that voice and do the opposite of it, and then we find ourselves with opposites, and we tell ourselves stupid shit like opposites attract.

When you don't show up for your assignment, you end up hanging out with the slackers who didn't show up for their assignments either. When you show for your assignment, the right people are there to work alongside you as well. That's a metaphor for every relationship. Work, home, children, spouse. Relationships with money. I want you to seriously consider what your assignment is. We all have an assignment. We all have that voice at the back of our head. Many of us try drugs and alcohol and everything else. We'll get with the wrong people because we're not listening to the voice. We'll destroy good relationships that we have. When the right person shows up, we'll do everything we can to fuck that deal up. We never really get in the true rhythm we were set out to get into in life.

I'm reminded of the story; an Australian fellow was telling it one time in a video I saw. A TEDx talk or some shit like that. He was talking about a plumber who was always singing. One day, the young plumber who was always singing fell off the ladder and broke his neck and went up to heaven. God was there. The guy said, "I was only 27 years old. I had so much more life to live. Why did I have to die so early?" God said, "I put you down there to be the greatest musician of all time, and you chose instead to be a plumber. I just went ahead and brought you up here because you were wasting the one life that I gave you."

It wasn't a deal about religion or heaven. It relates to God, or whatever this guy believed in. He maybe was a Tibetan monk for example. I didn't freaking check which nationality or religion. On the video, there was no distinction there. Whatever God he was paying attention to—you think about it—the guy basically wasted his life. God had given him a huge talent. The universe had given him a huge talent. Instead, he was dealing with people's shit for a living. You have an assignment. You've been given huge talent. The question is, "Are you dealing with shit instead of doing what you're supposed to do?"

Most of us don't think we deserve what we really are supposed to be doing. Oftentimes, I have to really remind myself, as we grow bigger, I've got to feel like I deserve this, or I've got to feel like I've worked for it. I work 10 times harder each day so that I feel like I've earned this shit so that I feel like I deserve it. If I wasn't working for it, I wouldn't feel like I earned it, I wouldn't feel like I deserved it. I would destroy it. It's the same way with any relationship.

Have you built up companies, built up employees, built up management, and everything else, and then you destroyed the fucking thing? Have you built up relationships, got engaged, planned a wedding, and then you bailed on them? Have you moved in with somebody and pledged to get married and you're going to be together forever, and you never even got a ring or you, never even moved forward there? Instead, you broke up? Shit happens. You have an assignment on you. Here's what you do. Once you find out that assignment and you know what that assignment is, and you get clear, and you listen to the voice at the back of your head, the number one questions you start to ask yourself are: "Are the people around me on the same mission? Are they part of this assignment, too?"

Guess what, if the people around you aren't on the same assignment, they're not on the same mission as you are, you're not going to get the mission completed. You're not going to be able to do what you're supposed to do here on Earth and, therefore, your life would have been wasted. I created you to be the greatest most talented musician to ever walk the face of the planet, and instead, you chose to deal with people's shit for a living. Are you dealing with people's shit? You need to ask yourself, are the people, places, and things around you that you have relationships with on the same mission you are? Are they going to show up for the same assignment you are? Or are you going to Iraq and they're going somewhere over in fucking Alaska to chill? Ice. Alaskan joke. You dig that, right?

You've got to take a firm stance of if they're on the train with you, if they're not on that assignment with you, if they're not on the same mission, you've got to let them go. The rest of the world is sitting here and telling you, "You can't bail on family. You can't bail on your friends. Don't turn your back on friends." I'm telling you right now, without being some cold-hearted bastard, those are the things that people say so that they can continue to do stupid shit and you'll forgive them. Listen, if you're one of those people and that offends you, hey, the truth shall set you free. It might piss you off first. On the flipside, the truth can set you free. But it will piss you off. If you always handle your business, if you always show up for your assignment, you don't have to worry about fucking shit up. You don't have to worry about all these people on the same mission with you. You've got to take a firm stance.

The rest of the world will tell you that you can't turn your back on family, but that's the part of the family with the weird uncle that still needs your help all the time. That's the little brother that can't get his shit together. That's the crackhead sister who keeps coming home with a fucking different dude every other week, talking about *this is the one*, and can't seem to get her shit together either. The mom who does nothing but sits around the house and watches *Jerry Springer* all day, smoking cigarettes, making you feel guilty for being successful. It's the dad who worked four years at the factory, and he only made $30,000, and what do you know, you're selling cars, making fucking 100 grand a year, but "You're probably ripping everybody off."

We keep these people in our lives, but they're not on the same mission as you. Much like that lion, you've got to go off on your own. It can be painful to cut ties with people you love. I'm three divorces strong. One time, I built up a decent fortune as a younger man, a couple hundred thousand dollars and cash and stocks and shit like that. I had been in the mortgage business and doing well. I went to federal prison. I got married to my girlfriend, fiancée, whatever so that she could control my estate while I was in federal prison. Two or three months into it, she's got another boyfriend, and she's leaving me and spending all my money, taking all my furniture, felt like it was rightfully hers even though she never worked. Tore my life apart, man.

It was really hard. Not because I loved her, that did suck, but because it was so hateful, such a fucked-up way to leave. It taught me a lesson. I trusted too much. I'm not saying don't trust people. I look back to that relationship, and I'm, like, I never let that person really earn my trust. I just gave it to her. Wife number one, I wasn't who I was supposed to be. I was pretending to be somebody else. She thought that I was the heir to all of this car wash fortune. She left me in a bad situation, too. Hit herself in the head with a frying pan, called the police on me. That's why you keep the cameras in your house. I beat the case; I had explained to them what happened. We had to go into a court, a jury. I actually won. It hurt for someone to do that and then put me through the process of having to go to court and hire a lawyer to defend stuff that I didn't do.

The next one left me while I was in prison. The third one left me when I was at one of my lowest-yet-best moments to breakthrough. I was just about to get really big in this Hardcore Closer thing. She bailed on me. Took my son from me, destroyed me worse than the one who took all my money while I was in prison because of Jax. I'll tell you, even at the age of seven, my dad gave up on me. Basically, broke up with me and let me be adopted by my stepdad like I explained earlier. Man, I've had some serious breakups in my life. I've had to cut ties with people who I really did love. I don't talk to my mom. I don't talk to my dad. My grandparents told me that if I wrote my book, we couldn't be cool anymore. My dad told me if I wrote the book, we couldn't be cool anymore.

They were ashamed of their mistakes. I wasn't ashamed of mine. I take personal responsibility for the mistakes that I made. I address those in the books as well. A lot of people want to hide their shit. Because they wanted to hide their shit, they were holding me back. I had to cut ties with them. Sad as it is. I miss them, yeah, absolutely I miss them. I had to cut ties with them for the fact of if I listen to these three people telling me not to write a book, then where are the people hearing me, reading my words? I've reached thousands of people. Maybe millions. All for three people.

I had to cut those alignments. It wasn't easy. How many of you aren't writing a book because your grandma would be ashamed of you? How many of you aren't doing daily blogs because your parents would tell you you're stupid? How many of you aren't posting about your business on Facebook because you've got two or three friends who say, "All you do is post on Facebook." That's all I'm saying. It's all relevant. You got to get rid of those folks. They hold you back. I had to get rid of people who I love the most. I had to get rid of people who probably had the best intention, trying to protect me, but just didn't get it. It's not been easy. Nothing worth doing ever is.

I grew up on a farm until I was seven years old. That's when I moved into the Dallas area. My grandpa owned the farm. As I've noted, he lost his business and everything else. We had to move from the farm. I think they sold it to somebody. I was a little young at the time. I lived on this farm, and occasionally, we had to kill animals. We had cows, and we would take the cows to the slaughterhouse. We didn't see it. We didn't do it right there on the farm or anything like that. Same with goats and chickens, we shipped everything off. It wasn't something that we did on site. Every now and then, you'd get a sick animal or a diseased animal or an animal that had been attacked by coyotes or something of that nature. You'd have to kill it.

Man, it was painful. I remember my grandpa telling me one time, "It's your turn. You got to be a man." I had to shoot this damn goat. It wasn't easy, but it was for the benefit of the goat and us because that one goat was going to potentially infect the rest of the herd. That one goat had fallen victim to the coyotes for a reason. Whatever it is. I can't remember the reason for why we had to kill it. For whatever it was, it ended the suffering of that goat, and at the same time, it was for the greater good of the whole farm. I'm not advising to go knock off your family members. Don't kill them at all. That's not what I mean. Even though that was a hard decision, a hard thing for me to do, I had to do it.

What I'm saying is, it's going to be very hard for you to cut ties with your family if that's what you've got to do if they're not on the same assignment. It's going to be very hard for you to cut ties with a significant other if that's what you've got to do if they're not on your same assignment. I have good news. I'll get to that shortly. Here's what happens first, before I get to the good news. We have this self-destruction. A lot of us think we're not worthy, subliminally, subconsciously. We attract bullshit, and then we get caught up in the drama; we get addicted to the drama. We go on this path of self-destruction as just part of the process.

I can tell you this. You can get back better than before. I'll give you a real-life example. Think of a person you might know or have heard of who was out of shape when they were with their significant other, and then they got a divorce, and she got really hot, or he got really hot, and started working out all the time? Why were you not showing up? You had what you wanted, and then you stopped showing up for it. Why did you do that? I know a lady who got divorced two years ago, now. She's down 60 pounds. She's gotten fake boobs and everything else. I think it's awesome. If you had that, you'd still be with your husband. Why did it take that self- destruction for you to get your shit together, for you to get your health together, for you to get your "snap back" because of the divorce? If you would have kept it like that and you would have shown up on your assignment every day, that divorce wouldn't have happened.

Just like in the medical business, people won't pay for supplements or workouts to prevent their health from declining, but as soon as you tell them they've got cancer, they'll pay you any fucking amount of money you want. They'll pay you whatever just to make it go away. It's the same with relationships. I'm going to help you out, though. I know it's been tough to get this information. You've got to cut ties with people, cut them off. Eighty percent of people are idiots. I guess what I'm saying here; we've got to keep this hardcore.

However, there's good news on the end of that. Once you start cutting ties, you start attracting the right people. It's not even about cutting ties. Once you start surrounding yourself with the right people, often the wrong people will run themselves off because they know they can't hang. My old friends don't come around these days and ask for no bullshit. They know better. They know they can't hang with the people that I'm hanging out with. It's not that they can't hang like "you can't sit with us." They just know their bullshit is not going to work because I've attracted people like me into my life. I have a family of origin that I don't really care much for, but I have a family of choice that I'd pretty much do anything for.

It's not because I've been monkey-brained or click-whirr-ed or any of that shit. It's because I've done what I'm about to share with you. There's a reason why the relationships I have work right now from my businesses to my business partners, to Amy, to Asher, to Jax, even Jax's mom. I was with Jax's grandfather today when I picked Jax up and took him swimming for a little while at the house. I had a couple of my friends and their kid over. Jax and Asher and Amy and I, we're chilling at the new house. When it was done, Jax's grandpa just lives up the street. Jack is there 90 percent of the time hanging out with them because his mom is always over there anyway. I took him over to their house and sat up there with my ex-father-in-law on the porch for a few minutes. There's no bad blood. I've made my effort and still shown up in my assignment in every way possible. There are no objections there.

Here's what I'm trying to tell you, I got there, and I have these people that I'm aligned with in the right way and the right decisions in life right now for a reason. The first reason is I became Ryan, the real Ryan. I had been pretending to be some other person my entire life. My identity was stolen from me at age seven. I'd been pretending to be someone else. As I'm pretending to be someone else, people show up expecting me to be that person. As they get to know me, they realize that I'm not that person and then we grow apart. What happened oftentimes, is that the click-whirr method kicked in, the monkey brain kicked in. Here I am staying with that person knowing I shouldn't have fucking been with them. They ended up staying with me knowing I'm not who they thought.

That's what happens in relationships. We're our best version of ourselves then we show up into the relationship. Then after a while, we get complacent in the relationship, and we stop being our best. Then something catastrophic happens and we start working to show up and be our best again, but it's oftentimes too late. Here's the thing about me. I just started being myself, who I really was. I was tired of pretending and attracting this fake person. Here's the agreement we have with people. If I'm fake and you're fake, and we get together, now we know both of us are fake. We don't want to tell other people that we're fake. Our agreement now is that we have to stick together because we know too much about each other. We have to stick together because we don't want to go through someone else discovering this about us. If you're fake and you attract fake, and they show up, and they're fake, then when shit gets real, neither one of you make it. Plastic melts.

Here's what changed for me. I started being myself. If I felt a certain way, I said it. I could be rude, lude or crude. I can be as professional as fuck. If I felt a specific way, I said it. I would rather this pain happen to me right now and find out that you're lying to me, find out your intentions, find out we can't do this deal together, find out we're not a fit, find out whatever it is right now than prolonging the shit for four or five years to waste my life only to find out at a later point what I could have found out right now.

I started setting those expectations, but I accepted them either way. If you're not this person, that's awesome. Here's the deal. If you're not a customer, you can't call my cell phone. That's not how it works. If you're not in The Tribe, you don't have my cell phone number. You can't just call me and ask me questions and run scenarios by me. If you're not in one of our high-ticket programs—that's part of it, having access to me—you don't get one-on-one time with me. I shoot the same way with the people who don't make the cut. I set the expectation, just like a sales process. Set the expectation. If they're not the right prospects or the right candidate, I accept them; I just can't be with them.

Listen, most of us have so many screwed-up relationship issues because we're not very selective. When we finally get somebody, we go all in with them, and then you look up one day, and you're like, "Who am I? I don't love this person. I don't love my life. I'm here; I have kids. I drive a fucking minivan." We have these thoughts. *How did I get here*? It's like boiled frogs. Have you ever heard that story? You take a frog, and you put them in a pan of water, it's lukewarm water. You turn the heater on, and it slowly warms up. The frog will never jump out, and he'll end up boiling himself. You throw him in hot water. It will obviously jump out. If you slowly raise it, it's not the same thing.

They slowly take away our laws here in America and probably

everywhere else in the world as well. You slowly reveal who you are. Over the course of a few years, they see the real you, and it's been this slow track record. Like, *shit, how did I get here?* Let me help you get through fear. A broken heart mends. What I mean when I say that is no matter what the fuck you're going through right now, no matter how painful it is to cut ties with somebody, you will make it through. We've all had a grandparent, or a great-grandparent die at some point in our lifetimes. We've experienced a parent, grandparent, somebody extremely close to us, die. We got through that. We got over it. Do we miss them? Yes. Have we made it forward? Yes. Was it the end of the world for us? No. Was it sad? Fuck yeah, it was sad, but we made it through it.

Stop fucking with people because if you stop fucking with people, they'll stop fucking with you. Most people will find that 80 percent of the people that you're surrounding yourself with right now, got to fucking go. I can tell you this. Once I kicked 80 percent of my network out, the 80 percent that I gained was the 20 percenters, 4 times over.

Once you show up as yourself, you get clear on your assignment. You get clear on who's on that mission with you. You get clear on who the fuck you are and what you came to do. You find someone on the same mission as you and those are the relationships. If you want to be the best real estate agent in the world, then you go find the best real estate company in the world, and you start working for them to become number one in their organization. If you don't, go to some shithole broker office that ain't got their shit together, and go work for them, thinking you're going to be the best in the world when nobody leads by example.

That's what we'll often do. I see guys selling Fords and Toyotas. You can make money selling Fords and Toyotas. I ain't knocking it. In a city like Dallas, Fords and Toyotas are a dime a dozen. Somebody selling a Lexus makes more money. It's a bigger price point. I see a lot of people selling $100,000, $200,000 houses who should be selling $400,000 and $500,000 houses. They're not in their assignment.

I challenge you this. Review your relationships. This is your homework. It's just like anything else. You can either do it or not. That's on you. How you do anything is how you do everything. Make the list of the top 20 people closest to you. The 20 people that you've spent time talking to, either it's real life, Facebook, in the office, on the phone, in the household. That includes your wife, your husband, your kids, your co-worker, your manager, your best friend on social media. Break down these 20 people. Look at those 20 people and ask yourself with each one of them, is this person pulling my hand forward, trying to get me to run with them? Or is this someone pulling my hand back, trying to keep me from outrunning him? These people trying to hold you back...you have to be honest with yourself. You've got to start finding a way to let them go.

The best way to let them go is going to be painful for you for a while, but it's just to replace them. Stave them out. Like I said, when I started surrounding myself with the people that I have in my life now, the old folks, the "haters" I had in my life, worked their way out. They're not around anymore. They couldn't hang with the new set of friends that I found. Sure, they told me, "You're into this Internet stuff. You're into this and that and the other." They tried. They kicked and screamed, "You can't..." Blah, blah, blah. Eventually, they found their way out. The way for you to do it is to start being yourself and to start finding some more people that are on your mission. You'll connect with them and what will happen is you'll disconnect with the 80 percent that you need to cleanse out right now.

I know it's a tough number. You look to maybe your best friend from high school who's on relationship number 100, still ain't never been married, is a hot mess, goes down drinking, gets fucked up every Saturday and then cries to you all day Sunday. You're over here trying to raise your kids and shit, man. Maybe it's time to let her go. Maybe it's time to let that job go, whatever it is.

This is the major key takeaway. Across every relationship, that you have, are you showing up and are you showing up as yourself? Sometimes we're showing up, but we're showing up as somebody that we're pretending to be. Are you showing up in these relationships as yourself? Because the only way that somebody can truly love you unconditionally is if they know the real you. If they know some fake version of you or some manufactured version of you, how could they ever love you? If you know some fake version of them, some manufactured version of them, how can you ever truly love them? Because you don't know them. Keep it real.

Make a list of 20 people you spend your time with and ask yourself these questions. Listen, if you're in the position you want to be in in life, awesome. Congratulations. That's great. If you're not, you really need to go through this exercise. You really need to see who's helping and who's hurting. I guarantee you; people are always doing one of the two. Remember that the heart always heals. Whatever relationships you have to cut, you have to cut. Listen, I went through three divorces because I wasn't being Ryan Stewman. As soon as I showed up as the real Ryan Stewman, I had Amy.

It's not even a fact of getting along. I've always gotten along with everybody. If I get a high, she's down low. These other girls were nothing like me. They were low energy. They weren't cut out for this entrepreneurial lifestyle. They come from families that didn't have it. Amy's dad was an entrepreneur. She's college educated. She was a hustler on her own. She's got it figured out. She's excited to work in our organization. She loves what she's doing. She takes pride in this. She doesn't complain about it. She steps up. She takes authority. Why? Because she knows who I am. I'm not out here hiding.

It's the same with the employees, the sales team and affiliates. We'll get on the phone tomorrow for our conference that we do on Mondays. When we get on there, I'm going to keep it 100 percent real with them. I'm not going to sugarcoat everything. They know who I am, so they want to work for the real Ryan Stewman, not just because we got this Internet thing going on. I'm talking about the fact that they want to work with me because of me being genuine with them. They know my pure intentions because I'm comfortable being myself.

It wasn't always this way. It took me a while to break out. I didn't just get divorced from Jax's mom and then was just like, "Nice to meet you, Amy. I'm this guy, Ryan." Totally reformed. I had to go through a transformation process. I had to go through an exfoliation process. I had to get rid of some friends. I had to get rid of my business partner. I had to do all that stuff. I had to go through and destroy some relationships so that I could make room for the right ones. According to science, humans can only have about 50 relationships. Some of those are online. The average person can only handle about 50 relationships. If you've got 50 relationships going on and 45 of them are bad family, bad work, bad kids, bad everything, guess what's going to hurt you?

All I ask is that you write down 20 people…see who's helping, who's hurting and what you can do to give them an exit strategy out of your life. Don't waste your life because you want to please other people who aren't worthy of being pleased. It's one thing to want to please people who have earned it. It's another to please them because your monkey brain has got you in some damn click-whirr agreement and you're miserable, and you're not listening to your vision, and you're in the wrong alignment. It's only a matter of time before you veer off the path.

The good news is once you become yourself, you start attracting the right people. Real attracts real. That's just how it works. Maybe not at first. It might take a while. Because people will say, "He looks real but he's probably acting real like so many people that act real, so we're just going to watch him for a while." Because real people don't just trust anybody automatically. Real people don't just show up and say, "Here, I believe you." Real people scope you out and see what you are about because they know what it takes to be real. It's not going to happen overnight. It's a transformation. The market, the other relationships, the other people that you have, they will see it. The good news is maybe one of your relationships you need to get rid of, gets mad at you and stirs up four or five other ones you need to get rid of, and they all go out together.

If you're living life to the fullest right now and you're enjoying this, that's awesome. If you're not living life to the fullest, don't short yourself on the homework thing. Do that. It will help you.

When I designed my perfect customer and my perfect spouse, I got clear on what it was I wanted. I got clear on who it was that I wanted in my life, who I wanted to align with. Then I focused on finding them. Maybe you should do the same.

Chapter # 7: Breaking Through Walls

Let's get into hitting walls.

But first, let's revisit the reason I've shared so much with you, and that's because I don't want you to just have this stamina, this energy, this feeling, this mentality for a short term. That's not the point. The point is for you to adopt this mentality and to make sure it lasts and propels you through a lifetime. You have access to this book. There's no reason you shouldn't review it once a year or twice a year. Every couple of years, I'll go back through the products I've bought.

I was moving...packing this weekend. I move on Tuesday. You know you pack, and you find a lot of stuff that you forgot about. One thing I realized about myself is I have a serious upper limit. I can see patterns of that upper limit everywhere.

As I was moving, I came across old programs, and I thought, "Man, I need to take this again. Now that I'm smarter, I can extract so much more out of this. Now that I'm aware of the first round, I can take so much more out of this book, this training program, this CD series or, whatever." My upper limit that I'll share with you is, I buy stuff. I make money; I feel like I've got to buy something. I get to making some money; I feel like I have to buy. I've got so much shit on Amazon that I'll never use, that's just sitting in boxes that I'm probably about to throw away as I move, that I'm embarrassed that I even own. It's not that I'm embarrassed because it's weird stuff. I'm just embarrassed that I've spent this much money over the years, buying shit that I don't even use, shit that I don't even need. Damn you, Jeff Bezos and your Texas entrepreneurialism.

I'm aware of this upper limit. I look for things like that in my life. I want you to start looking for patterns like that as well. Upper limits really tie into hitting walls. We're going to break through those motherfuckers.

The wall is a metaphor that people use when it comes to running marathons. People run a marathon, and they say around mile 15, you hit what's called, "the wall." The wall is trying to keep you from pushing forward in the marathon. It's that point in the race, that life, your muscles, your brain and everything else says, "You've done well, it's time to quit." It's not that you can't push through it. It's not that you don't have the endurance for it. It's that life starts telling you, the devil starts telling you that beautiful little lie about, "You've done good enough. It's OK to stop now. You're in pain. You've suffered long enough, my child." Your mind will tell you those lies.

The problem today in society is a lot of people listen to those lies. They take heed to those lies. They believe them. They're not breaking through walls; they're resting on them. They're using them as a place to prop up one leg and lean against, like Boomhauer at the beginning of *King of the Hill*.

What are the walls in your life? That every time you start running, you get on mile 13, you hit that wall? Let's identify some of those walls. I'll walk through a little exercise here in a second, but you need to start identifying what these walls are. When you know the "devil," is telling you that you've done good, that you've earned a spot to quit, you need to start identifying those spots that way you can look for it, and you can say back, "I've got shit to do over here. Don't put a wall in front of me. I'll kick the damn thing down. I'll hit it with a battering ram. I'm not scared."

What are some walls that show up in your life? Walls in relationships. Every time you get going good in your relationship, you start some unnecessary drama to run that person off. Every time your kid does well in school maybe gets an A on his report card; you find some way to balance that out. You hit a wall. You get mad and punish him. You know, the walls arrive everywhere. A lot of us…all of us business people, a lot of us will hit a wall in our business. The number one complaint that I get from the guys in The Tribe before they join The Tribe, of course, is, "I'm tired of having on months and off months." They hit a wall; they don't feel like they deserve two good months in a row. It's hard for them to fathom that. It's hard for them to push through.

When you're doing back-to-back months of consistency and commission in a commission-only position, and you're pushing through that stuff, it's much like a marathon. It's easy to run one month, do well and then, chill out the next month, right? It takes discipline. It takes stamina. It takes momentum to push through and do that every single month. It takes momentum, stamina, energy and most of all, mental toughness to be able to push through marathons.

I was thinking that sometimes mental toughness is something you either have or you die. Have you seen the movie—I forget the name of it—where the guy is jumping around on cliffs. It's James Franco. He's jumping around on cliffs in the Arizona desert. Something happens, and he gets caught on a rock. He has to cut his foot off to get out of the rock. That takes some mental toughness. A lot of people couldn't do that. A lot of people would have just died there.

I was thinking about that today because I saw a little preview or something on YouTube for that movie. As I was thinking about that, like, "It's amazing what you can do when you put your mind to it." You know when you go to the gym, and you see a certain set of weights, some weeks, you can hit a 300-pound bench press. When you've got that right mindset. When you put your mind to it. You go in there, and you're like, "Three hundred pounds is my bitch this morning." Most weeks, it's all you can do to hit the 250. You know? But nothing changes on the weeks that you hit the 300 but your mindset.

I thought, *there's plenty of times when I've been in situations, and I've had to lift objects*. I've had to do crazy amounts of things with strength. They say that if a mother's baby was about to be run over by a car, she could get so much adrenaline in her body that she could flip the car over. It's crazy, the things that we can do once we put focus on it. I've been in situations where I've almost fallen off ladders and been able to hold on for dear life.

I've been in situations where I've had to pick something off me or get something off me. Think about this, when you get in a fight, and you get someone off you, someone that's bigger than you and they're on top, you conjured up the strength to flip them over. We see it in the UFC all the time. That's extreme focus, what a lot of people don't have.

It's like everything that I've been saying as we go through these topics. How you do anything is how you do everything, right? If you're hitting walls in one area, chances are, you're hitting walls in all areas.

Why do you think walls show up? Take the time to identify where the walls keep showing up in your life but then ask yourself *why do they show up*? A lot of it has to do with upper limits. Walls show up as tests. When you're running a marathon, and you're on mile 13, and the wall shows up, that wall tells you, "Hey man. You've worked hard. You're on mile 13; it's OK to finish. You're good. Good job, buddy." That lie begins in your head. That voice in the back of your head starts lying to you that it's OK to quit. What's the deal there?

The body's born weak. We're naturally weak. In every religion, they talk about some sort of original sin that happened. Pandora's box. Adam and Eve. That made us weak. We're drawn by the flesh, right? The flesh is weak as hell. Our body's natural set is to operate the robot. All we are is wet robots. We're set to operate in our comfort zones. Magic things happen, we know, outside of our comfort zones. Our standard operating procedure is to avoid pain, seek pleasure and try not to hurt ourselves. When you're running, you're 13 miles in; things start to hurt. The operating system that runs our brains says, "Hey, things are starting to hurt. That's not normal. You've got to regress back to being comfortable. Let's keep you in the zone. We don't want you to get hurt. It's got to last you a hundred years. You were doing something that we weren't naturally prepared for."

That's why these walls show up. See, again, I'm referring to a lot of physical relations. How things relate mentally to physically. Again, when you're working out, you're sore the next day. You push hard; you're sore the next day. These walls show up when you're working out, "You only need to hit 250 today, so that you're not sore the next day." It's the body's way of saying, "Hey man, take it easy on me. I want to be comfortable." It's the subconscious' way of keeping you safe.

Here's the thing: Nothing ever happens in the safe zone. Nothing good, anyway. The safe zone's boring as hell. That's why people cheat on their significant others because nothing happens in the safe zone. It's not exciting. You have to test the limits. The only way to test the limits is to push through the walls, but you have to understand where the walls are and why they show up first before you can push through them. We suffer with this limited thinking telling ourselves *you've done good enough.*

I'll be honest; I look in the mirror, and I'm like, "Damn, how the hell did I let myself go?" I start looking back, going through the CATAPULT method, looking for that trigger. For me, 10, 15 pounds is a lot to be over my ideal weight. A) I'm vain as hell because I'm on camera all the time and B) my body does not store any fat, anywhere other than my mid-section. My legs don't have any fat, neither do my arms, or shoulders. Everything concentrates right there in my mid-section. It's the genetics. My whole family's that way. It can really alter my shirts and my pants fastening…it's annoying as hell.

I look back for that catapult, that trigger. This is just me being honest with you. I hate to even admit it. I realized that I caught hives about a year ago. I'm like, "OK, that got me out of CrossFit," because my head was swelling up every time I worked out. I stopped doing CrossFit. Then, I met Darren Casey, and we talked about those 30-minute programs. I thought I could do it on my own; I didn't pay him. I tried to copy his program and ended up getting a little bit lazier. Over time, I look back, and I'm like, "Well dammit, I was in peak shape, and I know what happened." I said, "It's OK man. You've worked really hard to get here, relax." Guess what? The body went back into its comfort zone, the normal operating mode. So, three months later, my little 15-pound difference is a lot to me. Since I added two inches in my pants.

I realized what it was that caused that limited thinking. That limited thinking was, "Ryan, you worked really hard for a year to get here. Take a break. Enjoy the fruits of your labor." Now, I'm going to have to work twice as hard, even though I'm still working out. It's not like I've been lazy or anything else. I just didn't really give a shit about my diet, switched my workouts from five days a week and an hour, to three days a week and 40, 30 minutes. After a while, stuff catches up to me like it would anybody else. That limited thinking is no different than the mortgage guy who closes 10 loans one month and two loans the next. "It's OK. You did a good job for a while. Take a break." That's bullshit because magic stuff doesn't happen on break. Nobody ever got a raise while they were on break. Nobody ever accomplished anything great while they were on break.

Here's why people hit walls. The walls show up because the subconscious talks to you and tries to get your brain into that normal operating mode. The reason why people hit walls and fail is because they believe the lies that they're told. Pain sucks. Nobody likes to have pain. Nobody likes to go through pain. They don't call it "growing pleasure," they call it, "growing pains," for a reason. There's no growth without pain.

The mental correlates with the physical. The supernatural correlates with the natural.

People hit walls, and they fail because they listen to that voice. I hit a wall, then a peak from CrossFit. My mind started playing tricks on me. Started telling me things that I believed. "Ryan, you've been working out every day like this for 10 years. Don't you think you deserve a break?" No. No, I don't. Nothing good ever happened on break. What I deserve is, now I have to step my game up even better. We move next week. I'll be in CrossFit again the week after next. It's time that I get my shit together; I've been on break long enough. I'm telling you as a person with an extreme amount of vanity. Me, sharing that with you, if I can be honest and open about that with you, hopefully, you can be honest and open about some of the walls that you're hitting yourself.

Everything's hard in the beginning. I'll make a video about this, this week, so watch for it. But everything's hard in the beginning. It gets easier as you keep pressing forward. It's easy when you start off running, mile one, mile two. That ain't shit. Mile 13 starts to get hard. Mile 14, you have to make a decision. Every day you're up against the mile-14 situation. You have to decide whether you're going to push through it or whether you're going to stay in the same place, revert back to your comfort zone.

It's easy for me to just sit over here and talk all this shit, right? It's easy for me to say, "Hey, here's the walls. Here's why they exist. You should push through them." I've been through plenty of walls in my life, too. Plenty of them have knocked me down. I'm not sitting here saying I'm some perfect human being. I've pushed through a lot as well. Usually, what's happened in my life, like most people who go through training, is I've had to hit the wall a few times before I learned to bounce through it. I had to be in wall-busting training. I'm a wall buster. One of those walls was relationships. I had to hit the...no pun intended, the wrong woman, three times, and get divorced three times before I finally learned to push through that wall, before I finally learned what it takes.

What I'd like to share with you in this next segment is how to fight that urge to quit when the wall shows up. This is why people are average. This is why people hate it when you remove their excuses. When you remove their objections when you show them what can be done, when you show them how you put in the work, and you've done the thing that they haven't done they get mad and hate on you.

The reason why they hate on you is because they chose to stop at the wall and you chose to push through. Maybe you stopped at the wall two or three times. Most people stop once and just take a smoke break for life. "Ah, fuck it. I'll just stop right here and smoke my cigarettes." Then, they get mad at the people who pass them up. "Oh, he's a brown-noser, climbing the company ladder." "He's only top producer because he got the good leads." We push through the wall of shit leads before you get the good leads. Even when you come to work at Hardcore Closer, we're going to give you some average leads. They ain't terrible leads, but we're going to give you average leads. The guys like Johnny and Roxanne that I know can close, get the good leads. It's no secret there. They had to push through the average lead wall first before I'd just hand them gold. They've got to learn how to deal with rubies before we can throw them diamonds.

You've got to fight the urge to quit. It all starts with learning how to push through pain. Tony Robbins, John Grinder, when they talk about NLP or Neuro-Associative Conditioning, what they're talking about is the human brain, the operating system searching for pleasure or pain. People are really motivated by two factors, pain or pleasure. They'll do things in search of, or in avoidance of, those two things. There are no shortcuts. We're making a decision about our weight. The pleasure of eating a candy bar versus the pain of eating some broccoli. The pleasure of eating a candy bar versus the pain of working out to reduce the calories that you took in from that candy bar. Most people will totally disregard the pain associated with those decisions. The workout, the calories, they never follow up with what they need to know and do, and they eat the candy bar. Here's why: Because that pleasure of eating that candy bar was more motivating to them; it was more appealing to them than the pain of gaining more weight.

There comes a tipping point in every relationship where all of a sudden, people say, "I've gotten to a point where I'm so overweight. I'm so unhappy with how I look. These candy bars are doing me so bad, I stopped eating these candy bars, and I'm going to start focusing on this pain. It's worth going through the pain." The thing about this, though, is that somebody will go through their whole life, smoking cigarettes; they'll eat like shit. They get diabetes, cancer and everything else and don't give two fucks until the doctor tells them that they're going to die. Then they'll spend all their money, any amount of money that they have to get better. Suddenly, they'll exercise; they'll eat healthy.

Plenty of people I know have lived a shit life until the doctor told them that they have cancer. Now, all of a sudden, they're fucking vegans and all natural, into yoga and have green juices and shit like that. I'm not knocking that, but I'm saying, their whole life they were on the pleasure of drugs. They were on the pleasure of everything that caused the cancer in their body. They got it from eating whatever they want. But nothing changed until the doctor told them, "The consequences of all that pleasure that you've been searching for are now pain."

What happens is a lot of people die of cancer. A lot of people die of heartbreak, suicide and everything else because they refuse to push through that pain. Let's take the show *The Biggest Loser*, for example. A lot of those people go through tremendous amounts of pain to lose massive weight. After they do, they have the operation and get all their loose skin cut off. They lose all their weight, and most of them turn around and go right back to it. They hit that upper limit. They haven't learned how to consistently push through pain. It takes an odd bird to be able to endure pain on a daily basis. It's someone weird who can go into the gym and totally push themselves to the max every day. Those dudes are ripped. Those chicks are ripped. We see them.

One of the ways to push through the pain is to get a coach who will push you through the pain. When I was at CrossFit, we had two coaches on us. "You can do it. Watch your form. One more rep! You're the man!" That shit goes a long way. You've got someone in front of you telling you, pushing you, motivating you versus that voice in the back of your head demotivating you, telling you that it's OK, telling you to stop. "Avoid the pain. Seek pleasure. Get into normal operating mode." You need a coach to counterbalance that.

In the gym, in business, you see why people hire me in The Tribe, and they pay $30,000 to be a part of our organization. One of the major reasons is because they need me in front of them going, "Oh, hell no. You had a good month this month; you better have a better month next month. Don't regress to the normal. Don't go into that normal operating mode. Go back. You made 50 grand this month, and you're going to make 10 next month. Ten doesn't even cover the bills or the operation that you've got going on over at your branch. The hell are you thinking? You've got to push and do 60 this month. No sleep til' Brooklyn. Shit, we're going further north. We're going to Canada." Brooklyn's a long way from Texas, for the reference there.

This is how you push through the pain; you find a counterbalance. For pain and pleasure, you find someone to push you through pleasure. "One more rep! It's going to feel great tomorrow. Run one more mile! Sprint just a little bit faster. Pick up the pace." In the back of the mind, in sports, life and business, your mind is telling you, "You've done a good job. Take a break. Calm down. It's OK, what you're going through; it's OK to eat this. Don't get out of your safe zone." When someone else is on the outside, who's louder than that voice inside your head, and they're saying, "Run faster. Another jumping jack! Push harder! Do another push-up! Sprint faster!" it's louder than the voice in your head.

Our monkey brain needs to be told what to do. The primitive

brain, which is how we mostly operate, believe it or not, creates patterns and habits. We only use about 30 percent of our brain capacity anyway. Most of it is what I call the "Monkey Brain." The monkey brain has to be told what to do. If you're running and there's nothing telling you what to do, then the voice in the back of your head starts saying, "Hey, there's pain. Shut it down." If you have a coach in front of you if you have a mentor in front of you, someone who can motivate you saying, "Don't shut it down! Hit it again! Make it hurt harder! Push through the pain! It'll be worth the pleasure!" that voice is louder.

Here's the reason why you should keep going and why that coach motivates you. It could be your spouse; it could be anybody. Hey, I'd love to be each and every person's coach. I'd love to see the entire Tribe in Break Free Academy. I know I'm coaching you right now. I don't want you to think I'm selling that. What I do want you to understand is, you've got to have somebody in your life whose voice is louder than the one in the back of your head.

Here's why you should keep going; here's why you need a coach with that voice, to be loud, to keep pushing you in the direction, it's because so many people hit the wall and quit. You want to be a part of the one percent. That's tweetable, right? So many people hit the wall and quit, you want to be part of the one percent. The one percent that kicks through that wall. The one percent that finishes that race. The one percent that has the mental toughness to endure the pain, knowing that the long-term result is pleasure. When you keep going, you have to come to the realization that most people have given up. They hit a wall. Their brain won't let them absorb any more of this good information.

It's no secret; we do it all the time. You've got to keep going. Here's why. I'll just tell you a story that will resonate with you. When I was young, I worked my ass off at this car wash for my stepdad. Doing so, he would always tell me, "One day, your hard work will pay off. You'll have my job, and I'll own this place." He worked there for 23 years and got fired. No pension. No retirement. A $120,000-a-year job. "You're out of here, buddy." No savings. He used to always tell me, "One day all this hard work will pay off, and you'll have my job. Maybe you'll even own the place." I showed up like it.

When I went to the mortgage company, my boss said, "Ryan, keep working hard. One day, all of your hard work will pay off." When I went through prison, people would send me letters, "Keep studying these books. Keep learning this stuff and one day, all this time and all this pain will pay off."

A month ago, as I left the penthouse in my Maserati to drive over to the new house that I was purchasing, I realized that that day's here. It's arrived. I'm almost 37 years old, and I've been working since I was 13, hearing the phrase, "One day, all this hard work will pay off." Now, do you think that's a marathon? Thirteen to thirty-six, you think that's a marathon? That's my mile 14. I pushed through it. I'm here to tell you that so many of my friends have tried to run the same race alongside me. They went back to that normal operating mode. So many old business partners, so many people that I know in my sphere of influence have resorted back to that old way. I kept pushing, and I can tell you that one day, it pays off. I'm living proof. However, my mile 13, my mile 14, it fucking hurt. If you were to equate it to running, I had already broken a foot, blown out a knee and fractured my hip and I still had to keep running.

There's a book you should read. It's called *Living with a SEAL*. It's by Jesse Itzler. Jesse's married to the billionaire founder of SPANX. Jesse is a hustler. He is a very, very stupidly rich, billionaire. Married to a billionaire. He's successful in his own right. He owns ZICO Water and all this other stuff. In the book, *Living with a SEAL*, he invites this SEAL to come live with him for 30 days and push him, to coach him to be in better shape, physically and mentally. At the end of it, he talks about the shape that he was in versus the shape that the SEAL got him in. For 30 days, he had to endure hell, but it was all worth it in the end. It all paid off in the end.

I'm here to tell you that I have wanted to quit plenty of times. The SEAL talks about running the ultra-marathon, which I think is like 90 miles or 100 miles. He fractured his foot and blew out his knee at some point and kept running and finished the race despite the pain. When you focus, and you have the right voice in the back of your head, if you can push through, it all pays off one day. The problem is, most people never work until that one day comes. They say, "Someday, all this hard work will pay off." A lot of times the voice in the back of their head is like, "You've worked hard all your life. Fuck it, it ain't going to happen. Go back to being comfortable and quit working hard." That's exactly what they do.

Even when you can't see it, even when you haven't seen it, even when people with 20/20 vision around you, in your life, can't see it, you have to understand that it pays off. Guess when it doesn't pay off!? When you stop. Guess when it doesn't pay off!? When you become average. Guess when it doesn't pay off!? When you do whatever everybody else does. The only way that you get paid above and beyond everybody else is when you do shit above and beyond what everybody else is willing to do. It will pay you. It will take care of you. It will be exactly everything that you wanted it to be.

In my life, I pushed through the wall. I have everything I want, the girl, the kids, the house, the cars, the money, the bank accounts, the business, the clients. I have it all. That which I do not have, I am well on my fucking way to getting it, proving that the work pays off. Here's the thing. Most people, never see that payday. They work their entire life hearing that someday all this hard work will pay off, only they had an upper limit or hit a wall somewhere along the way, and then they take a smoke break. How's this showing up in your life? Is it hitting home?

We hear that all of our lives, "It's going to pay off one day. Keep pushing, man. It's going to pay off one day. You the man! One of these days, all will come true." When I was first writing my blog, few people read my shit or watched my videos. "Dude, one day a lot of people are going to know who you are, Ryan. Keep pushing." Thank God, I had the right voices in my head. When people would say, "Hey man, this is some bullshit, you douchebag," I'd get rid of them. I don't want that voice. I wanted to be surrounded by people who can push through the walls. Nowadays, I get messages every day, "Hey man, I've been watching you for three years. It's exciting to see your success. I'm excited for you." These are successful people lifting me up, oftentimes and they've watched so many people hit that wall and fail, they're just happy to see one of them who's pushed through it. They're just excited to see another one of them join the club;

they're excited to see someone like them who finished the marathon.

Look at people who finish marathons; they're proud as hell! They put stats like 13.2 and 26-point-whatever on the back of their car. They hit the wall. Mile 14 fucked them over. Those are usually the people driving average vehicles, living in average neighborhoods. Hey, I'm not saying it's all about material things, you know that. What I am saying is, we didn't get here to live average in average neighborhoods and drive average vehicles. We came to live this life so that we can drive sports cars so that we can drive supercars so that we can live in mansions. Nobody as a little kid says, "I want to grow up and drive a Honda Civic and live in a Fox and Jacobs house." When you're a little kid, you say, "I want a race car, an airplane, a boat and I want a pony. I want to live in a mansion."

Somewhere along the way, mile 14 shows up in your life, whether it's in school, college, or real life. You start settling. "Well, you know, I did want a Lamborghini when I was a kid, but I'll take this fucking Mustang." "I did want a Lamborghini when I was a kid, but now I'm driving a minivan." I've got a kid myself. What you tell yourself is all excuses because you chose to hit a wall in your life. Listen, if you're still pushing and you've not got your Lambo yet, as long as you don't quit pushing, you will get it. I'm proof. I have the ability to get one right now if I want. Oh, I'm going to get one. When the time's right, I'm going to get one. Right now, the time's right for investing for me. It's nice knowing that.

I'm not sitting here bragging about money. I'm showing you that if you push, your hard work will pay off. You didn't start out in life wanting to be average. You didn't start out in life wanting to make 100 grand a year. "I want to be a 100-thousandaire." No. When you were a fucking kid, you wanted to be a millionaire. When you watched *Silver Spoons* when you saw *Richie Rich* or Orphan Annie with Daddy Warbucks, whatever it is that you grew up with, you wanted that. The reason why the Kardashians are famous is because they're rich as hell because they have that O.J. Simpson money from when their dad died. O.J. was worth like 50 million dollars; their dad took it all. They parlayed it into stores and making money. The only reason people follow them is because they're rich. If they were some poor hoes from the fucking projects behind me, nobody would follow them around with a camera. The fact that they are millionaires, that's what people look up to.

We didn't start out life wanting to settle. We didn't start out life saying, "I'm going to hit a peak when I'm 21 years old, hit a wall and drive a Tahoe for the rest of my life." Again, I'm not knocking minivans and Tahoes and shit like that. What I'm saying is, that's not what you set out to get. Make sure that that's not what you settle for.

Here's how you make that breakthrough. You've got to have the mindset of the man who won't quit. There was a man in the early 19th century who had this idea. This idea that no one else could even fathom. This idea that was so beyond what anybody else had thought of in the time. Did it seem not only inconceivable? It seemed insane that he would even bring it up. He stopped talking about it to people. He didn't want that voice in his head from those people, so he kept the secret to himself. Every night, he went in this barn, and he put in work. Decades pass. People in town thought he was not only stupid; they thought he was not only insane, but they also made fun of him because he had basically gone entirely broke, pissed off everybody, blown every connection, owed money all around town and was hated by most of the people in his life who knew him.

None of that mattered, he was on a mission to change the world, even if it meant stealing from somebody else and compounding their idea to make it his own. He was going to make it happen. He had the mindset of someone who did not give a shit what anybody else thought about him. This guy's mindset...he did not only not give a shit what anybody else thought about him...he was willing to do whatever it took to make his dream, his idea, come to life. He blew up his house. He blew up his barn. The neighbors had called the sheriff on him dozens of times. There were times when he wanted to hit the wall, of course. There were times when he thought *I'm never going to figure this out. I'm never going to make this work.* Somewhere around his 10,000th attempt at making his dream a reality, the light bulb came on...literally. Thomas Edison finally got the light bulb to work.

He didn't hit a wall because he maintained extreme focus, because he stole the ideas from Nikola Tesla and other famous people—Thomas Edison wasn't the true inventor of the light bulb, but he was relentless in his attempts to make it a reality. Let's respect him for that, whether you know the whole story or not. Because of that, you're sitting in light right now. You use the phone and electricity is a major portion of that. Now the things that used to remain unseen can be seen, illuminated. The path has been lit ahead for us because he decided he was going to do whatever it took, until the day that he died. And he was going to die if that's what it took, to be able to break through and see his ideas, his imagination, come to life.

You see, Edison understood something that most of us kind of know, that none of us ever really think about or take action on, and that's that everything is temporary. Even our stint of life is temporary. We're here for 100 years, and we're gone. We're nothing but like a flicker, "Dust in the Wind," like a Kansas song. Everything about us is temporary as well. You break an arm; you heal. You go through pain. It's temporary. It heals. It stops hurting. You go through a heartbreak. It's temporary. It heals. It stops hurting. You lose your parents. It's temporary. You heal. It stops hurting. You lose a job. It's temporary. You find another one. It stops hurting. Everything here is temporary.

Edison knew the pain of the townspeople calling him a fucking idiot, a retard, a dumb shit and a stupid ass, which created a massive amount of animosity toward him and the village people that he was trying to help by improving their lives. It got to the point that some of the stories told about him were mean and nasty. We don't know if they're true or not because we know people tell stories and there are two sides to everything. Edison was one of the most hated guys in his area, but he understood the mentality of: "That doesn't matter because as soon as I light these motherfuckers' houses up, they're all going to love me." This hate, this animosity, this rejection, this stigma that was on him, was all temporary because he knew when he pushed through to the end, when the light bulb lit up, and he could put that shit in people's barns, so they could see the animals better; and he would put that shit in their houses, so they could see each other better they would love him.

The light bulb led a revolution. Because of that, we could start taking care of our teeth. We started putting makeup on. We started trying to be more attractive. The light bulbs evolved over all this time. He knew that, and he became a hero as soon as the light bulb was ready. The temporary pain, even though it lasted through decades of people hating him, having animosity and judgment toward him, that pain was worth the pleasure of him changing the world. I look right now, out my window, at downtown Dallas. Buildings are green, purple and blue; it looks like Las Vegas down there. The Omni's got words drawn all over it. It's crazy.

All because one man decided to push through that 14th mile and endure the pain of being judged, being hurt and losing everything he had. He changed the fucking world because of it. He understood that everything he had to go through was temporary until it wasn't. Death's permanent. Once his invention took route and existed, it was permanent. We're temporary. The things that we create, the things that affect us can be permanent. The things that we have an effect on can be permanent.

Let's talk about where a lot of people get sidetracked. When a lot of people are doing something, they focus on the pain. "This hurts; so, I want to quit." "This is uncomfortable, so I don't like it." What I would challenge you to do is make a shift, immediately, right now, in this moment. Start thinking about the pleasure of things. "Oh man, that weight's heavy. It's going to hurt my chest." That's what a lot of people think. You need to think, "That thing's going to shape me into having a beautiful torso." Right? Center on the pleasure. "My wife will think I'm attractive by working out." "A man will think I'm attractive if I make myself physically fit." The pain of working out is worth having someone love me and love every inch of my body. The pain of going through a workout is worth the pleasure of my husband or my wife falling in love with me again like when we first met. I was in shape before I met them and decided that they were the wall that allowed me to let myself go.

Focus on the pleasure that you get from these things because it can drive you. The pain will usually drive you to quit. The pleasure will usually drive you to the finish. Oftentimes, that voice of pain is loud as fuck! The voice of pleasure is so far away, calling you. It's always far away. The pain's right there at all times. We walk around on this planet, and because of gravity, we have pain. Our feet hurt. Our backs hurt. We're one of the only biped species on this whole entire planet, and because of that, the way that gravity works on us is weird so, we walk around in pain at all times. We know pleasure is usually way off in the distance, but pleasure's over there going, "Come to me!" You can barely hear it because pain's going, "No! Lay it down, fool! Lay it down!" You have to focus on listening for pleasure. You have to focus on that distant voice.

You know, when I go for runs in the morning, I just kind of go in my zone. I focus on the music, which is the voice for me. I find my pace and go through my run. I hate running, you have to understand that, but I do it often, three or four times a week. I hate it. I fucking hate it, but I do it. I hate it so much that the voice in the back of my head's going, "No, fool. You don't have to run today. Sit down, Ryan." I hear the voice in the distance say, "Hey man, you're going to get back in shape, Ryan. You're going to get it all back together. Just keep running. You're going to look beautiful. You're going to feel great. Amy's going to be happy. People are going to look at you and say, 'You've got it together in every area of your life, financially, physically.' Just keep pushing, Ryan. It's what you want. You want to look in the mirror and be happy."

That voice is quiet. Meanwhile, "Stop running! Stop running!" That guy's loud as hell. He's right there in my ear. That's why I'm going to CrossFit, starting next week. I've got to get somebody in my ear louder than the voice, pushing me faster and harder. I'm focused on that pleasure when I'm running. I'm focused on that voice. I take three steps out of the parking garage, dude, and it's immediate. "Stop running, man. Stop running. Shut it down. You ain't got to work out today." My default mode starts happening, even more. Me, somebody who's been programming this shit into themselves for decades. Then, guess what? I hear that voice off in the distance, "You can do this, man. You can get everything you like. It's going to work your demons out. It's going to work your toxins out. It's going to make you in great shape again. This is how you create your energy, Ryan. This is how you return energy to the grid." That's what I focus on.

Here's another way to breakthrough. One time, I was watching an episode of *Sons of Anarchy*. It was about one of the black gang leaders; I forget his name, he was talking to one of the white biker guys. They've obviously had some race relations they were going through, that they're trying to work out. They want to be on the same team, but there's this whole race thing that they've got because of their prison connections. One of the black gang leader's guys killed one of the white biker's daughters. One of the white bikers shows up there to have a conversation with them, and the guy looks him in the eye, and he says, "Hey, man. I will have revenge, and I will take over every area of territory and your guns." He starts telling him this stuff.

The black gang leader looked him right in the eye; the black gang leader was way more evolved than these white hillbilly biker gangs. The dude was driving a Rolls-Royce. He had drivers with suits. Where the white biker guys looked like they all just got done cooking meth. If you've seen the show, you know what I mean. He said, "Turning pain into energy is king shit, man." What had happened was, because the guy's daughter was killed, he was fueled by rage. He turned that energy into seeking revenge against that person, right? He was right. When you can turn pain into energy, that's king shit.

People in your family die, and you use that motivation to make sure that you take better care of yourself so that you don't die an earlier death. That's some king shit. When your family was poor, and you starved, you used that pain of being poor and starving to fuel you into earning more money; you used that pain to propel you. That's king shit. Everybody wants to be the king until it's time to do what kings do. Kings have to kill people. Kings lose family members. A king's family members are targeted at all times for ransom. Everybody wants to be a king until they realize what it takes to be a king.

The number one thing, I believe, it takes to be a king is to be able to convert pain into energy. Many people convert pain into excuses. "Oh, it hurts, so I can't do it." Kings say, "Oh, it hurts, I'm going to push through it." The moment that you decide that you'll use pain for energy is the moment that you step into a new level that most people will never even fathom. You think, from my perspective, I've been through a lot of fucking pain. Divorce. Bankruptcy. Prison. Adoption. Massive amounts of pain and I've learned how to create energy. "Hey, man. Shut that shit down and use the pain to push forward." Some of us sick bastards, we get to working out or whatever, we start hurting ourselves, and we love it even more. We want to push harder. We've learned to create that pain and convert that pain into energy. That's king shit. Fucking king shit.

That's also how you break through when you experience the most pain in your life, just like the CATAPULT method I told you about in an earlier chapter. When you get to the most painful point of your life, that's the part you need to create into energy. I challenge you to think about what areas of your life are painful right now. How can you convert that pain into energy? There's a way to be an alchemist with whatever it is that's being thrown at you right now. There's a way to convert it. There's a way to take that pain and flip it into energy. You have to A) identify what that pain is, and B) see what the source of that pain is so that you can draw upon the energy that source provides. There's an energy toward pain. Pain has an energy. You've got to learn how to channel and convert that energy into your good instead of something that's come against you. You've got to convert and channel that pain into something that's for you instead of something that is against you.

Last, but not least, I'll share this with you. Every single thing I've shared translates over into every area of your life. I used the examples of working out and being physical. I think that makes the most sense. Most of us have seen a gym. Most of us do not like running. Most of us have tried or are working out, and we know that process. We don't want to wake up. We don't want to do it in the evening. We can understand that. That doesn't mean this was only about the physical ramifications. I'm not selling personal training. I'm telling you the things that I talked about in the physical also translate over into the mental side. They also translate over into hitting walls in your family, hitting walls in your business, hitting walls in your body, hitting walls in your bank account, hitting walls everywhere.

What you've got to do is channel that pain into energy. Listen, when it hurts on mile 13, and you've got to push through mile 14, you've got to figure out a way to take that hurt and fucking push through the wall. Guess what happens when you hit walls? It hurts worse. Have you ever run into a wall? Have you ever run through a wall? That shit is painful. You've got to sit down and turn that pain into power. We've all been there. We've all been on a treadmill. We've all been running. We've all done something physical where we're listening to the perfect song and then hit what's called a "runner's high." When you hit a runner's high, that is exactly what your body is doing. Your body is in perfect harmony, and it's converting pain into energy.

I challenge you to figure out where those pains are and where you can identify those runner's highs, so you can use them to your advantage. You can convert that energy, and you can have the shit that you set out to have. You can quit living the average life that you're settling for now. You can keep pushing toward those goals knowing that everybody in the town hated Edison. Knowing that everybody laughed at him.

Knowing that everybody said he was retarded and a fucking idiot and now, everybody is using his invention because he stuck to it and knew that their shit was only temporary. I challenge you to inherit and adopt that same exact mentality in every area of your life, not just physically but, mentally and spiritually and everywhere, in every other "itually" that you can think of in your life, as well, inherit and adopt that mentality.

The walls are going to show up every minute, every hour, every day of your life. It's up to you to identify them and push through them. I believe I've given you the skill set and the mentality to do that. It's up to you to make the shift.

Chapter #8: Happily Ever After

I'm living in a hotel with Amy and Asher. Jax is at his mom's. All my stuff is in boxes. The house isn't complete yet; it's a freaking stressful time, to say the least, right? At the end of this stressful time, I'll have a beautiful house, a perfect set up, a place that I can live for years. A place that I don't have to worry about landlords, people jacking my rent or anything else. There is a happily ever after picture to this whole house thing that I've got going on right now, but meanwhile, if I start thinking about what's going on right this second, it's like the floors ain't done, the paint ain't done. The crown molding isn't done; the doors aren't painted. The garage isn't converted. My study isn't quite ready. The granite countertops are missing from the kitchen. The guy said it's going to be another two weeks. Everything is going down, and I'm going to live in a hotel for two weeks. I had to go buy new underwear and new socks last night, not because I shit myself or my feet stink, but because I don't have any because they're in fucking boxes at my house.

Again, there is a happily ever after, when it's all said and done. The happily ever after is my kids get the perfect school district. Amy, my soon-to-be-wife, gets the home of her dreams. I get a silent fucking study area. I had the office framed in and installed silent walls, and glass. It's been painted. Dude, it's going to be so sick of a place to record stuff. The end result from all this is it's going to be perfect. It's going to be happily ever after. The thing is you have to go through hell sometimes to catch a break. I remember growing up in life, I would look at these guys, and I was like, "Man they are complete. Man, they do drugs. They do all sorts of dumb shit, and they never get in trouble for it." Then you look back later in life, and you see they turned out to be complete losers, and then you're like, "Shit, I'm glad I got mine out of the way early." All the guys or girls maybe in your case, who caught all the breaks, had this cool life. But you look up 30 years later, and they are like fucking Matthew McConaughey from *Dazed and Confused*. They just really don't have their shit together. They're hanging out banging the same young girls, or in most cases, they're not banging anybody at all.

I want to explain what happily ever after means. You know at the end of every movie, the curtain closes. When the curtain closes at the end of the movie, we don't know what happens. The guy gets the girl. The hero makes the rescue, whatever the case might be. We don't get to see everything that goes on after that. We don't get that part of the story. These Internet marketing courses and personal development courses are the same way. You get all this "how-to" stuff, and then you get to the point where it's fixed, and then nobody launches you out there, so how do you maintain it once it's fixed? How do you continue, how do you remain happily ever after because that's the important part? You don't want to be happily for a little while after. You want to be happily ever after. That's the goal, right? And I'll say even though I'm going through this stress right now; I'm a happy guy. I really am.

I get pissed off pretty easily. I have pretty quick mood swings. It's because I have a low tolerance for bullshit and because of the adverse situations I've been in. My fight-or-flight mechanism is strong toward the fight. I get tensed up wanting to fight. I don't necessarily mean physically. I'm not trying to go around being a tough guy, but when I get mad, I fly off the handle. You know, as entrepreneurs, we are passionate people. Passionate can mean we are really passionate and good at what we do work-wise, but unfortunately, passion almost always transcends over into our angry side as well, right?

Speaking of anger, I want to dig into living happily ever after. Well, first of all, I think if you want to know what happily ever after means, you have to know what happily ever after looks like. So, what exactly does that mean? Since we don't see it in the movies and since we don't get that in the Internet marketing world, a lot of people just don't know what happily ever after means. What it means is a perpetual state of happiness, an achievement. You've made this achievement. You've gotten what you wanted and remained there or better for the remainder of your life, for ever after. For us to do that we've got to figure out what happiness is. If you are going to live happily, we've got to discover that within ourselves; I can't do it for you. We've got to discover within ourselves exactly what happiness is. That's what I'm going to help you out with.

Let's define what happiness is because I think this is really important. There is an exercise that I call the perfect day exercise. I'm not the first one to come up with it. I'm not the last one to come up with it. Hell, I may not even be the first one to call it this name, but it's super important. I've done it. I make all my high-end, $30,000-a-year Tribe clients do it. I make anybody who comes through Break Free Academy do it, and it is a game changer. If you watch Core Influence, it's what Frank Kern asks you to do, but many people don't do it. A lot of people don't do the homework, so I'm going to explain it to you.

The perfect day is huge. It's a game changer because if you understand what happiness is, then you can pursue it. Have you ever thought about what it would be like if you had to live one day *Groundhog Day*-style the rest of your life, over and over and over again? What would that day look like? If they said you could have anything, any lifestyle, money is no object, no limit on anything that you could want, what would you do? Who would you do it with? Where would you live? Let's go through this because there are a few things that you're going to have to do. You're going to have to put a price on happiness because nothing comes without paying a price. Let's just be clear on that. In order to put a price on it, you are going to have to define it, so let's define it first. If you could live anywhere in the world, where would you live? Money is no object. Just do yourself a favor and grab a pen and paper or Evernote, if you're in the digital age like me, and write or type this out. What kind of house would you have? What kind of floors would be in it? What color would the cabinets be? What would the bathrooms look like? How many bedrooms would it have? How much would it cost? Put a number on the cost of that house.

If you say a million-dollar home, get clear on where that is because a million-dollar home in Ladera Ranch, California ain't shit; a million-dollar home in Dallas, Texas really ain't shit, but a million-dollar home in Wellington, Kansas is a freaking mansion. First, get clear on where you would live and then what your house would look like. What kind of cars would you drive? Would you drive Lamborghinis or would you drive Chevrolet trucks? Would you get a Maserati? I could vouch for them; they're cool cars.

So, what kind of car would you drive? How many would you

have? Would you have more than one car, and would that make you happy? If you could imagine waking up happy every day, what would you smell when you woke up? What kind of bedroom furniture would you have? Describe this shit. What does happiness look like to you because so many people are chasing happiness and they have no fucking idea what happiness is. If you don't know what makes you happy and you're pursuing something that you don't know what it is, that's called a wild goose chase where I come from in Texas. You know we got an old saying here in Texas, "You're being led on a wild goose chase," but it's true. How can you say you are happy if you haven't defined what happiness is? How can you say you are living your dream life if you haven't written it down? It's just like a goal. How can you say you hit your goal if you don't establish one? How many kids would you have? Who else would live with you? Would you have a maid? Would you have robots? Would you have a private jet? Would you have a small house?

Modest doesn't always have to be about big dollars. To each his own. Would you have some land with a bunch of rifles and shit, so you could doomsday prep? There are a bunch of options. What kind of food would you eat? What kind of amenities would you have? Would you have a swimming pool, a country club membership, season tickets to the Dallas Cowboys? Some of you right now are going, "Well, fuck no, I don't want season tickets to the goddamn Dallas Cowboys." Well, me either. Let's define what that perfect day looks like. Once you finish this book, you can go in and further flesh it out. The idea here is for us to put a dollar amount on what you are defining. A million-dollar house costs about $6,000 a month in mortgage payments. A McLaren cost about $25,000 down and $5,000 a month. A Ferrari Costs about six grand a month under the same terms. Put a number on your shit and use Google if you have to. Get as dialed in as you can because we have to put a price on your happiness.

We've got to define, what is it that makes you happy. Going on vacations often, taking care of your family, having more kids, buying your daughter a pony, whatever it is. Here are the things most people say: "You know, I'm just trying to be happy," but they are in the same position they don't want to be in, being sad, and they cannot figure out why things keep going wrong because they don't know what happiness is. I'm giving you a fucking gift. I'm giving you the gift of clarity because those who can see through the muddy waters, can get past anything. It's like when you have vision you can see through the muddy waters. I'll use a good old country example again, because that seems to be what I do even though I'm a city boy here in Texas, still a Texan. If you can see through muddy water, you can watch out for the alligators, the snakes, and everything else. It's the people who can't see through the muddy water who get attacked.

The problem is life comes at us with extremely muddy waters. We're not clear on what our happiness is. We are not clear on what our destiny is. We are not clear on what our purpose in life here is. We're not clear on what we should do for a living, how we should make an impact, how we can change things, what our significance is. We're not sure on any of that. When we arrive on this planet, it's muddy as fuck, not just for us, but for our parents, too. It's muddy as fuck. They don't know us; it's like this tiny screaming stranger was handed to people who have no fucking clue how to raise it other than what they've seen other people do and the water's muddy, real fucking muddy. Yet everybody walks around just assuming that they fucking see right through it, but the problem is, it's just like when people comment on the political posts. People say, "Oh, they're sheep. We have to be wolves. People going through the muddy water don't even realize that they can't get a clear vision for things. They don't even know what a clear vision looks like.

You realize that if an alligator gar lives at the bottom of the Brazos River, which is dirty as hell, red, and sandy and relies on motion to detect things; it doesn't know that that water's murky because it's never been to Cabo to see what clear water looks like. That's a metaphor for a lot of people living today. They've never had somebody mentor them. They've never had somebody share experiences. They are living in the muddy water; they don't even know clear, great-tasting water exists. If you were to take that gar out of that dirty-ass water in the Brazos River and you were to move him to Cabo, he couldn't survive in that clear water because what it takes to make that water clear such as salt, are adverse living conditions for it.

In other words, some people aren't meant to see outside the muddy water; that's why there is a one percent. Some people aren't meant to live in the clear water; that's why there is an 80/20 rule, but just like some people never make it out of the hood because they are not given the right information to get out of there, some people never get out of the muddy water. In both instances, some people just aren't supposed to get out because you can only get rewarded with the responsibility that you can be responsible and ready for. I guarantee you this, I have been to the Brazos River, and I've also been to Cancun, Cozumel and Jamaica, where the water's crystal clear and I prefer the crystal-clear water. I prefer the beauty of it, the look of it and there is nothing wrong with the Brazos River, but at the same time, now that I've had a dose of the clear water, that's what I want. I don't want to visit the Brazos River anymore. I did that when I was a kid when I couldn't afford to go to the clear water, but now I can afford to go to the clear water, so that's where I'm going. I'm headed to Pensacola here in another week, to the clear water. Not even on the bay side, we're going to the gulf side.

So many people are walking around in the pursuit of happiness with no idea of what happiness really looks like. Don't be one of them. I've given you a gift of clarity, and that gift of clarity will not only affect you in your home life, it will affect you in your business life. It will affect you in every area of your life because once you define and describe what happiness is to you, then you have a goal in front of you and then you are on the pursuit of happiness.

Let me tell you a story. Years ago, I was watching the Frank Kern Core Influence video, and I wrote down my perfect day, and I described my perfect customer. I lived that dream, even down to the woman I designed. I was with somebody else then, but even the woman I talked about and her attitude and everything else exists in my life right now because I got clear on what I wanted, so I was able to attract what I wanted. You see a lot of times, people aren't clear on what they want, and they act fake, and they can't figure out why they keep attracting the fake. Well, they say game knows game, right? Fake attracts fake. They are not clear on what they want; they think they want something else. They want what somebody else has and what they've seen somebody else has is fake as fuck, too. They don't even know what they want, and yet they complain that they don't get it. You see, not me, I was clear. I wanted three kids. I'm working on number three, practice as often as I can. I wanted three kids, all sons. That way I could start a TV show called *My Three Sons*, the new version, right? Just kidding, but I wanted three sons.

I mentioned that my wife drove one of the nicest SUVs that you can buy. Amy drives a Cayenne. I mentioned that I drive a fast car, I wasn't exactly sure of what the exact details would be because who knew how long it would take me to reach that perfect day, but I wrote down the details of the smell inside of it, and the way it made me feel anyway. The experience and the way other people looked at it are what matters to me in a lot of cases. I care about the way it reassures people that I am successful, so that's what I described in a vehicle for myself. Now I've got the Maserati Ghibli, a very respectable car. You see, I also had gotten clear about the alignments of who I would work with. Happiness means I'm working with this person, that person and we are doing this. I've defined that happiness for me in the future is owning specific kinds of businesses. I'm not at liberty to share that with you, but it's something that's very futuristic. Happiness to me is buying into these businesses and changing the world around me because I see the world changing and I know that you either get on board or you get left behind. And I know that I need to embrace the change now. I know that I need to be ahead because if not, I'm going to be left behind and I don't want to be one of those people.

You have to get clear on what a happy life looks like to you and once you get clear on it, guess what? Everything gets a lot easier. You know what to look for, but more importantly, you know what *not* to look for. That is how you live happily ever after. What it really takes is pursuing this goal until you get it. I'm living out my perfect day every day, but I'm still working on it. I adjusted it. I made it bigger. Now it consists of multiple houses, private jets, things that I didn't think of before. I wouldn't have any of this if I hadn't gotten clear on what it was that made me happy. Right now, I'm clear that happiness means 50/50 custody of my son and I'm on a relentless pursuit to make that happen because I understand that when it does happen, I'll be able to secure his happiness as well, which makes me happy. You know, I set my mind to meet these goals and I say, "If we do this, this will make me happy. If I do this, this is a piece of my happiness puzzle." If I like something, I make the tweak. "Yeah, that would really make me happy. I'm going to add that there," but I'm clear on what it is that makes me happy. And that's all I focus on. It keeps me optimistic. It keeps me motivated.

A lot of people are clear on exactly what their fear is. A lot of people are clear on exactly what could go wrong. A lot of people are clear on exactly what could happen if they take that risk and they wonder why shit keeps happening to them because that's what they are fucking clear on. You see the real fucking magic happens when you get clear on the right things at the right time. The right shit happens. It's just like those murky waters. A lot of people don't even know what clear water looks like, what an alternative looks like for them and they're focused on the negative. They're focused on the things that could happen.

They are focused on the things that could go wrong instead of the things that could go right and the things that they do want and the things that will make them happy. Then the things that go wrong, the things that don't go right, show up continuously over and over and over and over in their life. And they become pitiful, and they become powerless, and they whine, and they cry, and they complain, and the bottom line is it's because they were clear that that was an outcome for them.

So, the universe dealt them that outcome. They were worried about gaining weight, so much so that they gained weight and then they think, *well, how did I gain weight? I was totally conscious of it. I was worried about it. I knew it could happen.* But you were fucking clear on it, that's why it happened. You weren't clear on staying skinny because that's what really makes you happy. You were clear on the fear of gaining weight, and not that happiness that comes from staying thin.

It's all in the mindset; it makes a big difference. It really does. Again, it's overlooked. A lot of people swimming in muddy water never had a taste of the good stuff, and they're not sure what happiness looks like. They are just doing life. Just aimlessly wandering the desert like Caine from *Kung Fu*. As we close, I want you to finish up this book and then actually do the exercises I talked about. It's imperative that you get them done. If you cannot define who and what it is that makes you happy, you will never find happiness, and that's not me being negative. That's me keeping it real.

You know, I bet you can look back over your life, and you could see every incident where you worried about something happening, and you worried it into existence. It's weird how our minds can do that, but I want you to look back and realize that you can use that same power to worry the right things into existence because the power of focus is unlimited. The power of words on our subconscious is huge. My guess is you've probably spent a lot of your life worrying about the negative shit. You're not trying to be a negative person, but maybe you have concern for your job crashing, and then it does—fuck. You have concern for maybe your family falling apart, your marriage falling apart, your kids not liking you and then it does. I want to challenge you to change your perspective, the way you talk, the way you walk, the way you think. And instead of focusing on things from a negative aspect, focus on seeing things from a positive aspect. Instead of worrying about getting fat, concern yourself with staying skinny. Instead of worrying about losing your business, concern yourself with growing your business. Instead of worrying about losing your wife or abandoning your kids or your kids hating you, focus on making them happy and keeping them. It will make all the difference in the world in your life.

Take the next 45 minutes or more to write down your perfect day, then put a price on it, so you will understand the price of happiness. Then go do what you have to do until you can reach that level. Guess what? You might think, *man it might take me all my life*. If that's what you're focusing on, that's what's going to happen. You need to say "OK, here is my dollar amount, $1.9 million is my dollar amount." Maybe that's yours. Say $1.9 million is my dollar amount. This is how many sales I have to make to hit that $1.9 million. Here are how many people I have to talk to, to make that many sales. Here are how many leads I have to generate to talk to that many people. Here are how many dollars I have to invest and what systems I have to have to generate those leads. Break it down and get clear, and you will live happily ever after because you know what that looks like, and that it feels like because you'll have a taste of the clear water; you won't want to go back to the Brazos River.

I am dead serious when I say, spend the next 30-45 minutes writing all this stuff down, and getting clear on it. Put a price tag on your happiness and pursue it.

My goal is for whoever is reading my words, that I hope it will change your life in some minute way at the minimum. I know what I've introduced you to have been major keys and have given you a lot of great insight.

Thanks for reading, and don't forget, I have other shit for sale that you should buy, too. On HardcoreCloser.com, look under the products tab, and you will see all sorts of stuff that will help you get the money that you need to become that happy person. Put the price on your happiness. Buy my products. Invest in my programs. Come join The Tribe. Come to Break Free Academy.

We'll help you make that money, so you can reach that level of happiness so that you can obtain what it is that you deserve.

About the Author

Ryan Stewman personifies the underdog story. He was adopted at age 7, expelled from school at 17, in prison by age 20, in prison again by age 26 and divorced three times by the time he was 35 years old. Despite all these setbacks, he's created the ultimate life for himself. He's a family man, proud father of three boys, CEO of multiple successful businesses, founder of a tech company, best-selling author, social media influencer and contributor to *Forbes*, *The Huffington Post* and *Entrepreneur*. Ryan resides with his family in Dallas, Texas. This is his fifth book.

Made in the USA
Middletown, DE
07 August 2022